How Not To Be Hacked

The Definitive Guide for Regular People

James J. Deluccia IV

To Loren, my family, my friends,
and
to Mr. Michael Hamelin, who taught me so much and left us too soon.

CONTENTS

CHAPTER 1

A PRIMER ON OUR CONNECTED WORLD

TIPS IN THIS CHAPTER:
- ✓ Why this matters to you and your family
- ✓ Protecting your life, family, and information
- ✓ When to take action
- ✓ How you can use this book

Technology permeates and enhances our lives on many levels, but too often people fall victim to online criminals. In this book I have set forth best practices in a concise and complete format. It is your definitive guidebook and reference point for how not to be hacked.

This book is perfect for anyone who uses technology. Adopting these tips will reduce your vulnerability to criminals and increase the speed at which you recover in the event that you are hacked. To understand why all of this matters, please continue reading this chapter. If life is calling, feel free to jump around using the table of contents to immediately solve your current needs.

WHY THIS MATTERS
How do online criminals steal your identity, cost money, hijack your medical benefits, and delete your files ...and how can you fix it?

This is a complex question that has prompted national conferences and inspired an entire profession dedicated to finding answers, but frankly, there is no magic answer. Maximizing the benefits of technology while minimizing the risk of being hacked simply requires adopting a few new habits.

In school you were not taught the benefits or practices for living in a fully online connected world. You were taught 'Stop, Drop and Roll', 'Don't talk to strangers', and 'Only you can prevent forest fires'.

This book is for you, the everyday person – not just for the techie, or the professional, or the information security specialist. Using technology and living our digital lives to the fullest can bring great joy to ourselves, opportunity to others, and care to those in need.

This book is full of simple habits that will enable you to enjoy the technology of today and tomorrow. This is not a book about giving up on technology, cutting up your credit cards, cancelling your social media account, or living off the grid. I assume you want to live on the grid and embrace technology.

To accomplish this goal each tip is presented in a manner that addresses the most common situations, and eliminates specific situational differences that introduce undesired complexities. If you are interested in more detail and options, please visit the website and discussions for greater depth or peruse the proceeding pages where the ideas are expanded. The Tips are structured as follows:

- Tip! – a concise description of a new habit for you to adopt.
- Greater detail and some technical info that are helpful for the more complicated concepts, as applicable.

These tips are based on the most effective behaviors, but not all possible behaviors. If you follow these tips you will be far better off and experience less real $$$ costs and frustration. Of course, feel free to jump around! If you are going to travel - check out the travel tips; if you are banking on line - check out that section. Keep these tips nearby when you sign up for a new service or purchase a new gadget. These are tools to empower your family, your friends and you.

Every tip includes a meter showing Low, Medium, and High. Each of these ratings is related to the type of protection benefited from the Tip. Protecting Life, Family, and Information are designated for each tip. Together you will be given the knowledge on the probability of this being sensible to adopt. An example is below:

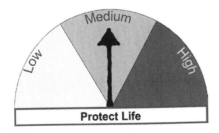

PROTECT LIFE

These tips directly relate to attacks that can cause physical harm or psychological harm to ourselves, our family, and our friends. These tips and the situations they address center on where technology is used by evil individuals. These were carefully considered and marked to raise attention to these situations.

PROTECT FAMILY

These tips defend against historically successful criminal attacks that impact you, your family, and friends. The damage may be that their devices are physically lost, digitally trashed, and or can include you causing and family financial harm too. These tips help prevent the source of the problems from affecting your loved ones. Certainly their information is at risk here, but that is not the end game. The criminals are after your family and friends to broaden the damage that they can inflict.

PROTECT INFORMATION

Finances, personal details of information that when combined publicly with other information, such as found on a social media site, can result in financial loss, privacy, and fraud. The frauds could easily consist of identity theft and bank fraud. The principal motive here is financial gain by the attacker, so the targeted information is for accounts online, financial banking details, and information that'll help acquire those financial assets.

As technology which could affect your personal well-being arise, I will continue to publish cutting-edge research and tips on hownottobehacked.com. My first tip for you: go to the site now, bookmark it, and add yourself to the mailing list. This will ensure you receive updates as they come about and are published. If you prefer Facebook, please follow me at www.facebook.com/hntbh.

As always, any feedback and ideas are welcome. Simply email or send a note from the website.

YOUR MONEY AND YOUR TIME

A large portion of the tips in this book focus on how to minimize or eliminate the expense and pain associated with protecting your finances against fraud. Fraud globally is a $11.27 billion problem globally[1], and results in five cents for every dollar spent.

There is often confusion regarding WHY we should care about this information. Some will say, "I don't care who knows I like _____, or who knows my phone number. There were phone books before today and how is it suddenly bad for that information to be public?"

The WHY is time, money, and physical well-being are at stake. I'll directly address each of these without introducing fear, uncertainty, or doubt.

WHY CARE ABOUT YOUR INFORMATION - TIME:

Recovering from identity theft will consume up to 400 hours of your personal time. This includes time to identify the problem, research and determine your next steps, contact the business(s) involved, place phone calls to and file claims with the FTC, IRS and police department.

The loss of personal information and identity theft is a permanent event; once this information is stolen and used maliciously there is a very high probability of the same previously stolen information from being reused for criminal advantage to you in the future. These future identity thefts are from criminals reusing your stolen data from old breaches and any news ones. It is fairly simple to get a new credit card with a new account number;, but you cannot replace your birthdate, birth city, family member names, etc. You will spend up to 16 hours per incident to clean up the simplest events, and more time when personal information (beyond just username & password of a website) is stolen.

WHY CARE ABOUT YOUR INFORMATION - MONEY:

The average cost to an individual who must clean up a fraud / identity theft is $800 per event and the average amount of fraudulent charges is $1,600 per incident - according to research released by Javeline

---

1   Nilson Report, Archive Graphic on Card Fraud 2012, link

Strategy and Research in 2013. According to the U.S. Department of Justice Bureau of Statistics, The amount of damages increases, to $2,183 when the person is a victim of more than one data breach[2]. This cost continues to increase as our dependency on technology increases.

Mean, median, and total losses attributed to identity theft and property crime, 2012

	Mean	Median	Total (in thousands)
Identity theft[a]	$2,183	$300	$24,696,300
Property crime[b]	$915	$150	$13,991,700
Burglary	2,378	600	5,234,800
Motor vehicle theft	7,963	4,000	3,079,900
Theft	447	100	5,677,000

Note: See appendix table 6 for standard errors.
[a]Based on 11.3 million persons 16 or older who experienced one or more incidents of identity theft with known losses of $1 or more.

Some frauds use your credit line to buy houses, cars, or time shares, and others are aimed at redirecting your 401k and government checks. How long would it take for you to realize someone cashed out your 401k? Six months?, A year? This is not just about the cost of the event. A lifetime of savings can be threatened.

WHY CARE ABOUT YOUR INFORMATION - HARM:

Losing time and money is one thing, but some frauds attack medical history and benefits. Identity impersonations have caused allergies, medical histories, and prescription histories to be modified. In one published case, the medical history of a patient who was allergic to penicillin was altered and the allergy deleted, this "hack" was life-threatening.

---

2   U.S. Department of Justice Office of Justice Programs Bureau of Justice Statistics, December 2013, NCJ 243779

THESE TIPS ARE THE KEYS TO SAVE THE INTERNET:

While there are many benefits to us for implementing these tips there is also a greater good to consider. When we protect our identities, finances, and computing systems (smartphone, tablets, computers) we prevent them from being used by criminal and rogue nations. Those who wish to do evil take advantage of inadvertent weaknesses in behavior to finance crimes and conduct espionage that will harm your quality of life.

Criminals who install malware on our devices can use our devices to harm others. The act of commandeering 10 or 20 million computers (unbeknownst to the owner) to cripple a business or service (such as the New York Stock Exchange, FAA Air Traffic Control, Microsoft Xbox, or Netflix) is a real and imminent threat to our way of life. At a minimum, implementing best practices makes our lives safer and could reasonably be considered the neighborly thing to do.

WHEN SHOULD YOU TAKE ACTION
TIMING

Most of the tips here are focused on an event or activity, such as going on a trip. However, there are a number of tips from which you can benefit if you complete them on a recurring basis. These are highlighted for your convenience, and I hope you will take these to heart. The tips which have a recommended timing or recurrence are designed to 'clean the slate' of any prior mistakes (by ourselves or those who have access to our data).

EVENTS

Events are things like buying a new phone or a taking a trip to Italy and I have used these examples throughout the book. The new gadgets provide a fresh start which means new accounts, privacy settings, and application of the tips found in this book. You do not need to memorize what to do when you receive a new gadget, but instead leap to Tips that apply to your new gadget – simple! From the good events (new gadgets and fun trips) to the disappointing criminal fraud (data breaches, malware on computer) you can similarly leap to the sections that address each moment in your life. Of course, you can always revisit these on an as needed basis to help make for an easy refresher. In addition, you can adapt these habits to your own personal situations!

NEW DEVICE

Adding a new internet-connected device (i.e., phone, digital streaming TV/radio, health-fitness tracker) is a perfect time to set up your accounts securely and manage settings on your new devices. The tips that discuss online account management, passwords, and two factor authentication (explained later in Chapter 4) will definitely be helpful.

It's not you who I don't trust, it's whoever will have my data next (i.e., 3ʳᵈ parties, Mergers, bankruptcy, criminals)

WHY NOT TO GIVE YOUR PERSONAL INFO TO EVERYONE FOR A QUARTER; THE RISKS; THE PRINCIPLES

First Principle - the person who is receiving your data (cashier, cute teller) can cause us harm simply due to human error; everyone makes mistakes, or the individual you hand your credit card to may be manually or electronically copying your card data to sell to buyers of stolen card information. Credit card information is not the only thing that has been stolen during the course of business. There have been cases where medical office and/or hospital staff have sold medical records. Unfortunately, much of this is beyond your control. So we want to reduce the amount of information we provide to third parties as much as possible. Be observant here.

Second Principle - the cute teller who received your data transfers it to the merchant/business. At this point you have ZERO control over it. Certainly there are laws, ethics, industry standards and scores of people working at all hours to safeguard the data, but there are an equal number of criminals pursuing that data. Consider that in nearly every case, the information (credit card number, social security number, email) you provide to one business will be stored, processed, and managed by many other businesses.

Very often, through mergers, acquisitions, bankruptcy, data breaches, and human error, our data is gained by people or companies with whom we have no direct relationship. That is why most of this book focuses on being resistant to harm by addressing Second Principle situations.

A NEW MINDSET – SMALL TOWN VS. INTERNET CONNECTED
Trust between two people is not the same as trust between two computers

Many of the risks relate to the possibility that there is something erroneous in the computers involved which then leads to these personal difficulties.

I love speaking to friends and members of each generation (Gen X, Gen Y, Millennial, Baby Boomers, and so on) about trust. The members of each generation have specific levels of immediate trust with each person he or she meets. Some go forward with complete faith in humanity and have been wronged on only a few occasions. Others are much more cautious of the average person they meet. These levels of trust make sense when proximity and involved parties in this trust model.

Those who lead with immediate trust are typically applying this trust to persons who they meet on the street (in their neighborhoods), or in the store (in their hometowns), or anywhere else nearby. Statistically speaking these are generally not the criminals we worry about, and more to the point this population is likely exactly like the trusting person in question (same upbringing, culture, income bracket, and on). The guys of Freakonomics would have a field day on this implicit trust concept. (Visit Freakonomics.com for a wealth of writings and media on behavioral data)

It is possible that someone in this neighborhood will collect your data and harm you. The likelihood of this happening is very low, though. That is not the case when our data, financial, health and other personal information is shared on computers. This is because the information is permanently exposed to a massive population set which is absolutely different from the hometown described in the example above. Worse, the data shared is rarely if ever deleted, so it is like playing Russian roulette without stopping after five rounds. Not a good idea!

Knowing that our data is possibly exposed at some point to a much larger population that includes criminal actors is the reason for the *new requirement of not leading with blind trust.* In most cases we can and should trust the merchant, charity, or individual with whom we are doing business electronically. The caution that must be applied is that we are not only doing a transaction with that specific individual. Instead, we are playing a pass the message game with our credit card, but unlike the game where it is hilarious to see how different the message is from the beginning to the end, the financial details remain the same and make theft easier.

Say you tell your computer and the application (web browser or App on your phone) that you want to buy that 'basket of flowers' for your mother. Your computer then passes that information on to, on average, 19 other computers and applications to convey the message. Now visualize yourself sharing your 'basket of flowers' order and credit card number with the next 19 people you see in traffic this afternoon. What would be your comfort level with that practice? Likely not high, but even if that isn't the case hopefully this illustrates the fact that it is not one transaction alone. There are people / computers / software between us and our desired recipient who we don't know, and we don't know what they will do with our information.

Being aware of these risks, these systems, the concept of the 'passing the message game', and facts surrounding the Implicit Trust Bias related to population size will enable you to be more prepared in using computing systems securely and safely. So here is our first tip:

If you adopt the tips in this book you will be a superhero, poised with confidence and knowledge to prevent digital harm.

Let's get started!

CHAPTER 2

CREDIT CARDS AND SENSITIVE INFO LIFE HABITS

TIPS IN THIS CHAPTER:
- ✓ Never using your debit card
- ✓ Swiping credit cards
- ✓ Sharing least information at check out

Did you know that over the last few years, so many businesses and government bodies have been hacked that 70% of U.S. population[3] has been exposed to criminals between December 2013 and February 2015[4]?

What is striking is the low amount of relative fraud given the vast quantities of data available. This reality is of course of no fault of your own, but like getting caught in the rain – wet is wet.

In addition, we as citizens operating in the world of credit cards and online finance systems must practice smart habits when engaging in this world in order to be responsible stewards of our identities. This section provides tips for handling important documents, credit cards, and general good practices.

The tips here were gathered, reviewed, and improved upon by

---

3   United States Census Bureau. https://www.census.gov/popclock/

4   Privacy Rights Clearinghouse https://www.privacyrights.org

professionals from leading financial institutions, leaders in the cyber security space, and special investigative units from the FBI.

This section will give you skills above and beyond the common person and make you more resilient to criminals – in the physical world and even more so in the digital.

#1 Don't ever use your **debit card** again

DEBIT CARDS VS. CREDIT CARDS

In your wallet there are two types of cards: a credit card and a debit card. Both allow you to make payments to a merchant. One places you with all the liability and the other limits the liability. Therefore a simple principle can be offered:

Never use your debit card for purchases.

- Consider cancelling it completely
- Use it only physically in person at an ATM
- Ask your bank to only link your checking account to ATM card
- When making purchases, use your credit card only when cash is not available.

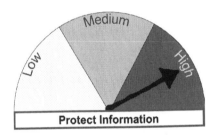

DEEPER THINKING

An ATM card (that which we use to access money through teller machines) and a debit card are different products from the bank. You can certainly have just an ATM Card and avoid the associated liability of a debit card.

In the United States this protection is established in Federal Law that applies to Credit Cards. In case of a loss from a credit card fraud you are only liable for roughly $50, total (most credit card companies waive the liability fee)[5]. The loss possibility is orders of magnitude larger victims of debit card holder victims.

---

5   The Fair Credit Billing Act (FCBA), 15 U.S. Code § 1643 - Liability of holder of credit card

#2 Swipe the card yourself

Whenever possible, don't hand your card to be swiped but instead ask to do it yourself. This is becoming most frequent and familiar with the Chip readers found globally and adopted in the U.S. in late 2015. It is not always possible, but when available it is the best option.

This applies when you are at a restaurant, retailer, or really anywhere. This is a cultural norm across Europe, so when traveling it is an anomaly to actually hand your card to someone. In other parts of the world it is more likely someone will take your credit card and swipe it for you.

If you are holding the card there is less opportunity for the card to be copied.

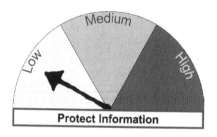

DEEPER THINKING

The concept of swiping will slowly disappear as new technology appears, but please keep this safeguard in mind even as it becomes rarer. A classic way in which fraud is committed is through what is called skimming. This is simply the process of copying the credit card data. The copying can be done at any point after the card is handed to a stranger.

Criminals can accomplish this in a retail setting by copying the magnetic strip with a handheld reader. A less sophisticated method is for an individual to write down the printed numbers on the credit card. While less sophisticated, this works just fine.

There are other methods of course, and some are quite elaborate. The act of skimming can also happen if a criminal installs a reader on the machine itself. This can be done unbeknownst to the retailer (as has been the case with retailers and some gas stations).

#3 Always use credit cards, and preferably provide as few personal details as possible

It is best to use a credit card when making purchases in a physical store. The check-out process sometimes feels like 20 questions, and you need to challenge the need for these details and opt out when possible.

In addition, there are new methods of paying for goods using services like PayPal or your iPhone. These options are all equally good as long as they are linked to your credit card or a fixed amount of money in an account without being linked to your bank accounts.

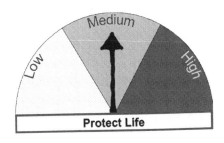

CHAPTER 3
PAYING FOR GOODS

Today you can buy just about anything, from anywhere, using any form of payment method that is convenient. This flexibility has been introduced by technology and is the building block for our connected world. The flexibility introduces a set of considerations that have not existed previously.

Consider that when you pay for cash in person how direct and final that transaction is in that moment. You know what you are receiving and you can only use those physical bills one time. If you lost a dollar, you knew you lost it, and it is gone. In the digital age – your credit card, Amazon account, Apple Pay / Google Wallet enable the transfer of your money, but are not in fact money. These technologies online allow for high speed transactions across a vast number of environments – craft fairs, retail establishments, and the Internet.

'Digital transactions using these payment methods suffer from a similar risk:

- Credit card numbers are the same, every time and for all transactions

- The username and password to buy something on Amazon and Apple is the same for every transaction

This means that if that information is known by an attacker, it can be used for their own purchases. So instead of the single use effectiveness of a dollar bill, we have a supremely more efficient method of transacting business that can be used multiple times at high velocity. Therefore new behaviors are needed to ensure that you benefit from such efficiencies, and not be the victim of these same benefits.

#4 No electronic transfer services attached to your debit card

As the first tip emphasized the value of using a credit card over a debit card – the same advantage exists to you for NOT connecting / registering your debit card to any electronic transfer services.

These are services that allow you to transfer money – large and small sums of money to other individuals. While each innovation of products are different, fundamentally they enable simple direct transfers of money based on phone and email accounts. This is currently being done by startups using simple SMS messages, email, plastic dongles, and full service websites. The reason to avoid these is the risk to losing the financial funds within that attached bank account. The same risk that exists in general for debit accounts.

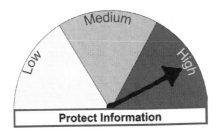

These services are very good and in most cases more secure than common card technology. The best way to use these financial electronic services is to load money onto the system or connect through your credit card. This will ensure you are protected in case a criminal gains access to your account.

#5 Never pay for goods with a check or bank account online

Online transactions are set up to make it very easy to purchase the goods we desire. At the checkout part of a website you are often given several options of how you'd like to pay for your purchase. Never pay with a check or by providing your bank routing numbers - <u>NEVER EVER</u>.

In cases where that is the only option available you should mail in a check because you are most likely at a government website, or someplace that shouldn't be selling online. Most banks allow you to use the bank website to send the merchant/government/person a check directly – this is by far a safer option and recommended in this case.

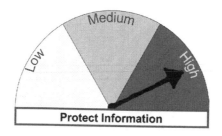

MORE REASONS!

Giving your bank account details, as mentioned previously, is a horrible idea. This is the direct line to your money without the amazing fraud prevention in place designed for such online purchases. When purchasing something online and there are other options available always choose a safer option. This is true for government websites/services and common companies. The cost of a stamp for postage is significantly more appealing than the possibility of your bank records being exposed and the trouble involved with bank account fraud.

#6 If you receive any message asking for account information (banking, passwords, etc...), **beware**

Every bank on the planet states that they will "never ask for your account information online or via email, ever," yet this is one of the most successful methods of attack used by criminals.

–It's simple. If you receive a note requesting your credentials, NEVER provide them and NEVER click on a link in such a communication no matter how scary or professional it may sound.

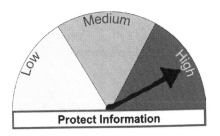

Protect Information

REASONS

Online service providers like banks never ask for such information because they already have it on hand. Therefore they are never going to ask for it in the most insecure channel ever created: email.

If you do receive such a message follow the tips shared in this book go directly to the business website to log on, and see if there are any actions required. If there are it will be clear.

Rest easy; some things are simple to avoid.

CHAPTER 4

PROTECTING YOUR MONEY ONLINE

TIPS IN THIS CHAPTER:
- ✓ Two-Factor, free and effective protection
- ✓ Safely transferring funds
- ✓ Preference towards guest at check-out

Money online is equivalent to physical currency only in that they represent the same value. You can exchange one coin or bill for X product universally the same online as you would in person physically. When you lose a physical twenty dollar bill it is gone. The same is true online, except online accounts typically contain **all of your** twenty dollar bills (think of your savings account or the maximum withdrawal amount available for your 401k). The net effect is far worse with online money accounts and exacerbated with the simplicity and quickness of online transfers of money.

Criminals love attacking bank accounts because it produces the greatest reward for the least amount of (their) risk. Crimes against our financial accounts can happen at very high speeds – most bank accounts can be emptied of $500,000 or more on a single Friday afternoon and made unrecoverable due to foreign bank deposits by Monday morning.

So it is particularly important to protect yourself against attacks on the accounts storing your cash. The tips here focus on a few specific and proven safeguards. They are widely available for all of the payment methods recommended.

#7 Use 'two factor' authentication for every account that has MONEY in it

For each of your accounts that involve monetary transactions, you should use two-factor authentication. This applies to:

- PayPal accounts
- Amazon accounts
- Bank accounts
- BitCoin accounts
- Stock trading accounts

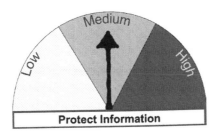

The type of authentication offered by each provider varies. . A nice online resource to see which businesses support two factor authentication can be found at https://twofactorauth.org/

"Two factor" authentication, is your best line of defense if you want to protect a financial account from being emptied in a four-hour period.

MORE DETAIL

"Two factor" authentication is best described as "something you have". This means that when you log on to your bank site you are asked:

- What is your username (not secret)?
- What is your password (something you know, but discoverable)?

The password is commonly referred to in the information security field as the "first factor". By implementing two-factor authentication, you introduce the "something you have" into the equation which could be any of the following:

- A series of digits sent to your phone via text message
- A small application/device/token that shows a series of ever-changing numbers

Requiring this additional authentication for accessing your accounts reduces the risk of harm and fraud. The majority of social media, banks, financial sites, online retailers, and technology companies offer two factor authentication for free. Charging for this feature is rare but is occasionally used for corporate accounts.

#8 Set up 'two factor' authentication when you move money

Every financial institution supports (for free, in most personal account cases) your ability to set up and require two-factor authentication when you request to transfer money. Use it. You should set this up with the following institutions now:

- Personal bank accounts - including checking and savings accounts
- Business bank accounts
- Credit cards / Loans / Mortgage accounts (because these accounts allow you to withdraw cash!)

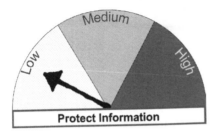

TECHNICAL DETAILS

- "Two factor" authentication for transfers of money will save you headaches into the future
- Setting this up will require you to navigate your financial institution's website to ensure alert and verification through two factor occurs

#9 Purchase as a guest if making a one-time purchase

Imagine if you had a key ring in your pocket with a physical key for every store you visited at in the past five years. It would be huge! In fact, I venture to guess you would need more than one pocket. So, when buying online, instead of having to manage and protect accounts at web sites you only occasionally use, choose to purchase as a guest. This is a common option at most good sites.

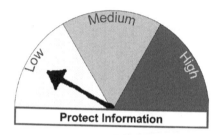

WHY?

This allows you to reduce your account management activities and the flow of email as well as limit the number of places where your credit cards information is stored online. Of course, this requires you to keep a record of the transaction should a dispute arise related to the purchase.

If you become a frequent shopper, by all means sign-up, you'll perhaps receive perks and at minimum will simplify the effort required for each purchase.

#10 When in doubt, pay using a credit card, and... in that order

When in doubt, pay using a credit card, PayPal®, Apple Pay™, Amazon®, or BitCoin, in that order. Given there are so many options to pay online a lot can be confused as to which method is the best. While every individual's situation can effect what is the "best", there are options that at large are the best. These are the recommendations I make to family and friends. The subtle difference of each is balanced against the risk to you, the fraud prevention safeguards, and their convenience factors.

When you buy something online please rank your payment method options in the following order:
- Credit Cards
- Apple PayTM
- PayPal®
- Amazon®
- BitCoin

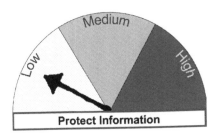

The rationale behind this ranking covers different aspects of security, fraud technology, authentication, liability, and legal components. The simplest explanation for this prioritization though is that these options are the farthest removed from your actual bank records and they create a limited liability and a ceiling of loss.

Credit cards are by far the most widely accepted and have a history. This history provides consumer protections, established procedures in case of a breach, and a bit of centralized that allows for easy cancellation.

Apple Pay is a great method of payment as you centralize your bank/credit card information with a single provider. If you have ever purchased an Application for your device then you already trust Apple with your financial information. By using Apple Pay while shopping, the retailers do not get your information and therefore you are limited of breach to only one provider. Amazon is similar to Apple Pay in that only Amazon has your information and the retailers that operate off of Amazon.com do not gain your details. Again simplicity is your friend.

PayPal has a proven deep fraud prevention technology, allows for centralization of payment transactions with a large variety of online retailers (more than Amazon and Apple). This is primarily an online only method.

BitCoin is an electronic currency and should be treated like gold. Meaning that each BitCoin that you have is usable only once, and once you use it in a transaction the next party physically possess it. This means they can be stolen like gold, but there is huge advantage in the extremely low probability of loss from a retailer that is breached. Use with care, as this is a fairly new method of making transactions online.

CHAPTER 5

USE EMAIL SAFELY

TIPS IN THIS CHAPTER:

- ✓ Disarming malware attachments
- ✓ Don't click on links
- ✓ Never email personal or financial details

Email is just like regular postal mail, but the cost of sending an email is zero. This allows everyone and anyone (including criminals) to send emails to anyone they like as often as possible until they achieve their goal.

There are a few things to consider with regard to electronic messages (email, text messages, online chats):

- Anybody can send an email, just like anyone can send you a letter
- The sender of the email can be real or fake (I have seen many a letter from the North Pole)
- A message attachment can hide a virus that poisons your computer
- Links ("Click here!") in messages can allow an attacker to install software on your computer or share your personal information
- Email Spam / malicious email = ~65% of ALL email sent in 2014[6], it's not personal ... these attacks are automated and criminals are playing the numbers game

6   Kaspersky Lab's email traffic analysis for 2014, URL, http://securelist.com/tag/spam-statistics/

- "Playing" a recording, watching a video, or viewing a page sent from criminals increases the likelihood of your system being infected
- Beware of false notifications – in email programs and chat programs, these are designed to hit an emotional reaction

#11 Don't open attachments in email, chat, or on phone without notice

A common tactic used by online criminals is to send a picture, file, or Microsoft office document to a victim. The attack is successful when the individual clicks/opens the attachment.

At this point the attacker can automatically install a virus, backdoors, and begin to steal private information (i.e., tax, bank, or medical information) from you. This attack, called Phishing, is at the most basic level exploiting human response behaviors. So - do not open attachments you received unless you asked for them or were given notice.

My preference when I receive such attachments is to do the following:

- Review the message (sender name, email, and message) to see if it is consistent with a discussion I have had with the sender
- If yes, then I have my antivirus scan it (Google and others can do this automatically if the file is attached)
- If it is a LINK to a file, then do not click it – instead, write a NEW email message to the sender and ask about the link

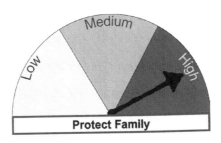

Why suggest you not open a file you have received from a friend or family member? A valid question. The basic premise here is we are trying to protect ourselves from an attack where our friend/family member's account is impersonated.

Remember, it is not the person we don't trust, but those who may have his or her credentials or access to his or her system. Email addresses can also be spoofed (faked) to trick you into thinking someone you know sent the email, instead of the bad guy/gal. Therefore when we receive files, links, and references that are out of context or unexpected we must treat them with a bit of caution. This hesitation and evaluation will reduce the probability of an attack by over 50%.

OH NO... I OPENED THAT FILE, AND IT WAS BAD, NOW WHAT?

1. Close the program opened by the file attachment
2. Confirm your anti-virus / malware software is up to date, and run it (this may clean it up)
3. Write a new message to your friend who sent the file, and alert them about the message (typically these are sent without their knowledge, because their computer account is hacked)
4. Do not use this machine to access financial accounts for a few months, just to be safe
5. Strongly consider restoring your computer from a recent backup, especially if your computer starts behaving badly

(Behaving badly – symptoms include: your email/social media accounts posting random messages, unusual pop-up windows, increased number of advertisements, and a slower computer)

If you did get infected from this file, please revisit Tips #6, 31, 61, and 63 to help protect you.

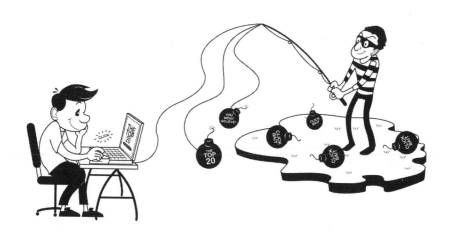

#12 Don't click on ANY links you receive!

When you receive an email or text message from someone and it contains a link that you did not request, you should NOT click on it. You should only click on the link if you were expecting that link, or confirmed the integrity of the link with the sender.

This is a very strict rule that applies to **all messages**. The intent here is to protect you from links that will install backdoors, viruses, and other nastiness on your device (to include: smartphone, tablet, and computer).

So, if you purchased a product from a website and then receive an email to track it would pass our test: you reasonably expected to receive the message and a tracking link is also reasonable.

If you randomly receive an e-mailed link from a friend or business it would not pass our test: You did not request the link, it is odd in its nature, and the message doesn't fit the author's style. In some cases the criminals are quite creative in their messages, so please be mindful.

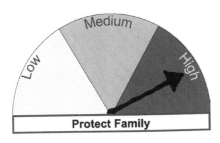

DEEPER DETAILS

Phishing is a type of fraud where an attacker sends a target (you in this case) a message that may sound very convincing. It may appear to be from a family member or your bank, and may include many personal details. This message will contain a link and you by nature will want to click on it. Except now you won't, and as a result will not become a victim to this fraud.

If you are unsure and wish to explore the link further, a simple test is to Google the URL, link, or keywords and see what is in the top 10.

Most phishing attacks that occur are aimed at more than one person, so it is likely that a discussion on the URL or link is happening online. A simple review of the topics of discussion will enlighten us as to the validity and integrity of the link in question.

Another example: If a link is offered from your bank type it out manually in your browser instead of clicking the link within the email. This way you are certain to reach your expected website. A simple link, can lead you to site which impersonates your bank's site (banks are most commonly impersonated due to the easy next step of stealing the money from the account).

Clicking on any link in a fake/evil email can compromise your device's security, your privacy, and that of your friends.

MOST POPULAR MESSAGE SCAMS BY CRIMINALS

Email scams:	Classic subject lines: "Your Order...", "Your package" "Jury Summons Fine...", "Order Confirmation"
Chat scams (i.e., Facebook Messenger / Google Chat / others):	Enticements: Scammers try to trick you with fake offers of free, rare, secret or exclusive digital goods Warning signs: Random request by new 'friend'; All friends receiving the same message Classic phrases: "Watch urgent...", "Saw your picture..."
Phone text message scams:	Enticements: Promise of free gifts, like computers or gift cards, or product offers, like cheap mortgages, credit cards, or debt relief services to get you to reveal personal information. Warning signs: Phone App store opens asking to install application, or device updates (all bad)
Social Media post scams:	Enticements: Special deal or exclusive offer Warning signs: Requirement to update video player or add software to browser; Obscure links and post by individual; rapid amount of links shared; advertisements Classic phrase: "Watch this..."

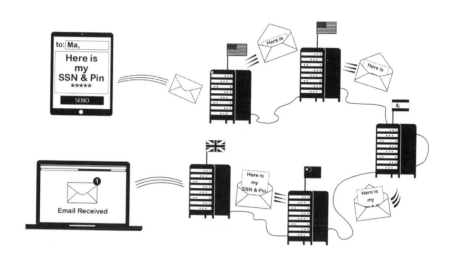

#13 Never email personal details or financial information

Email is not secure and should never be a method of sharing personal details such as Social Security Number (SSN), Date of Birth (DOB), Credit Card numbers, and passwords. Financial information such as usernames, account passwords, your secret PIN, and of course actual account information should never be sent via email.

And NO, you cannot recover from breaking this rule if you delete the email VERY fast. Once it is sent it is exposed forever. Remember, it is not that we do not trust the intended recipient, but instead we don't trust the 19 computers and hundreds of persons who have access to that transmission.

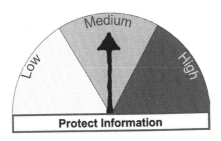

A BIT MORE DETAIL

Email is a fantastic way to share ideas and exchange messages. It is one of the worst methods of sharing sensitive information. This is due to the number of points in the email ecosystem where there are computers, individuals, and archived information that can ultimately fall victim to attacks by insiders and criminals.

Simply keeping this data out of email is the best and most cost-effective method.

CHAPTER 6

GETTING ONLINE - USING PUBLIC WI-FI AND KIOSKS

TIPS IN THIS CHAPTER:
- ✓ How to use public & free Wi-Fi
- ✓ Safely using Shared Computers
- ✓ Kiosks, the petri dish of computers

Public systems are very useful and convenient. These are specialized systems that help us automate activities and bring the convenience of computer where we may not have one on hand. These are great at movie theaters, airports, train stations, and of course at hotels (checking in). There are also Internet Cafes where you can go to access email while abroad. In most retail stores you see Internet-connected computers that many use to access their personal accounts.

These systems though must be considered as if they are SHARED dishes that the last person before you used without washing, and that has happened at least a dozen times before you arrived. Kind of gross, and that is precisely how you should feel when using these systems.

The digital junk, malware, virus, cookies, and prior behaviors are all piled up on this public system and therefore we need some healthy habits.

#14 When using a public Wi-Fi connection, confirm details with the provider

When traveling around the world or visiting establishments down the street it is convenient to use local Wi-Fi for connectivity to save on cellular data costs, but be sure to ask an employee of the business where you are connecting for the Wi-Fi name and any password details.

Criminals set up fake hotspots at popular travel destinations and they can be easily avoided by simply asking for the name of the legitimate network and password. In many cases these are posted by the cash register.

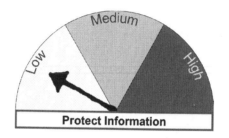

#15 Do not access your bank website from a public Wi-Fi

Coffee shops and parks that offer public Wi-Fi are incredibly convenient and suitable for just about every online activity. However, you should never access any of your financial websites - savings accounts, checking accounts, 401k, or credit card sites from such places.

These sites should be restricted for the privacy of your own home or a more private location, such as your office. Accessing these sensitive financial sites in a public Wi-Fi setting puts you and your money at risk and increases the probability that your information will be stolen and used by attackers to steal your money. Be aware this applies to any device – smartphone, tablet, and laptop.

- The risks can be summarized in three general categories:
    - » Over-the-shoulder surfing
    - » Recording of your username & password over the air
    - » Inadvertent sharing of secret passphrases
- The probability of these things happening varies widely depending on geography, Wi-Fi location, and the individuals around while you accessing these sites. The highest threat locations are typically high foot traffic, such as:
    - » Tourist centers (cafes and internet kiosks)
    - » Airports
    - » Taxi stands and train stations
- When you MUST access these sites in high risk areas:
    - » Use your smartphone with Wi-Fi turned off (cellular data plan) to 'do your business'
    - » Use a Virtual Private Network (VPN) personal service

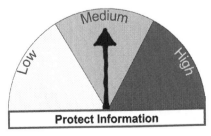

#16 Do not log onto email, social, or bank accounts from shared computers

Shared computers can come in the form as free iPads (available from most airlines), demo computers at stores, special use devices, and more! Providers of shared computers aim to offer machines that are clean and free of malware (such as keystroke loggers that send every key stroke you make to a criminal server) and other such personal safety risks. Unfortunately these systems are publicly accessible and there is a high chance that your data may be recorded and be used to cause you personal financial harm.

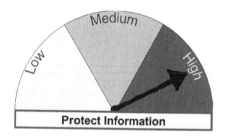

Thus, if you must use these machines use them sparingly and for a particular purpose only. Using these systems for anything non-personal is great (so therefore, no signing in to email, bank accounts, social media, airlines, work, etc...), and to be clear shared computers are ANY public system, and include:

- Shared computers are found at internet cafes
- Transportation venues as already described
- Computer store demo machines (i.e., Apple & Microsoft stores)

The risks that exist within these systems occur because the systems are public and susceptible to all the ills the Internet has to provide. This means the system has been exposed to every person before you, and all the sites, files, personal preferences, and bad behavior is what you are stuck with – basically a petri dish of malware, virus, spyware, and key loggers.

Remember that these systems are not your own. When you search for a store near your home address on your personal machine that information stays with your machine and web browser. When this is done on a public kiosk it stays with that public computer.

#17 Kiosks are public machines, and so is the data you give it

Kiosks are great as a special purpose devices as they can have elegant interfaces and provide simple functions, such as picking up movie tickets; printing airline boarding passes; ordering tacos. These can be hidden in plain sight, but include the following:

- Some Kiosks you shouldn't trust:
    - » Hotel lobby computers
    - » Internet Cafes in malls
- Some we don't have a choice:
    - » Airport check-in kiosks
    - » Train station machines (subways)
    - » Movie theater machines

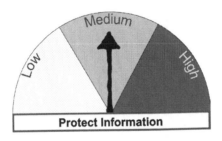

We must use what's available when certain situations arise. When using these devices, be mindful of your surroundings and ensure the device you are using is the official system and not a third party kiosk (For example in some European train stations there are ticket machines outside that transact through a third party company, but if you buy the tickets at the train counter or inside these systems are direct with the train operator and therefore have less risk). When forced to use these systems, consider the following tips:

- Cover the pin pad with your palm or other item
- Observe for modifications – such as loose wires, broken security tape, or disarray
- Use your credit card vs. debit card on these systems

CHAPTER 7

HOW TO BROWSE THE INTERNET

TIPS IN THIS CHAPTER:
- ✓ Never use Internet Explorer®
- ✓ How to stop spying of your web browsing
- ✓ Logging out of sites
- ✓ How to answer 'challenge response' questions
- ✓ Simplifying where NOT to browse on the Web

"The Wild West" that is the way to think about the beauty and openness that is the Internet as is known today. To appreciate the Internet it must be appreciated that it was designed to be as de-centralized, independent, and flexible as possible. When it was designed it was done so to ensure that communications could occur if a part of it was destroyed or lost.

These attributes though also mean you as the explorer on the Internet need the best mode of transportation and simple appreciation of the world around you.

- Given you can navigate anywhere online and view anything you want, you need to be sure that the your vehicle (web browser on phone or computer) is capable of handling the data being shared
- The web traffic you create from point A to point B can be maliciously modified unless you are careful and take precautions
- Not all websites NEED the "real" answers to the questions

they are asking, but instead are looking for you to help them create a personal and direct relationship – unless you are on a government run site, be mindful of the details shared

Remember the connection between you and the web site you are interacting with has up to 19 different machines involved and each is trying to protect you. To minimize your risk; increase your personal security;, always seek to reduce the number (i.e., avoiding Kiosks if possible) of systems involved and the sensitivity of the data (i.e., not giving all your private data) shared online.

#18 Do not use Internet Explorer ever again

There are many web browser options available to you as a user of your computer, tablet, phone, and other devices. Elect to use a browser other than Microsoft's Internet Explorer if you use a computer running any version of Windows®.

Good alternatives include:

- Google Chrome
- Firefox
- Safari

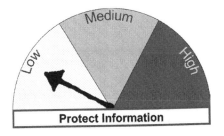

A common risk to users exists when the web browser developer and the operating system developer are from the same company. As of April 2015, Microsoft operating systems made up over 90% of the desktop computers online[7]. Therefore the simplest recommendation for the regular person is to not use Internet Explorer. Beyond this risk there are quantifiable details of life of vulnerabilities and time to patch that emphasize the importance mixing up your web browser choices.

This is a hotly debated topic for many within the information security space and the arguments and reasons to support each specific browser have their supporters and critics. This recommendation is based on two decades of experience, analysis of millions of system security results, presence of malware, frequency of attacks, number of vulnerabilities (think of vulnerabilities as open doors on your house

---

7   NetMarketShare Realtime Web Analytics, visited May 2015, URL

that you thought were locked) per browser, and time between patches (think of patches as installing new locks on the doors that actually work) by the vendor for each browser.

The simplest and most quantifiable factor is the time between discovery of a vulnerability and the time when it is patched. Chrome, at last analysis, patched discovered vulnerabilities in half the time of Microsoft Internet Explorer (IE); this means that in 2013 every Internet Explorer user was vulnerable for an extra 15 days after the patch was released and again in 2014 a study[8] showed IE as the most vulnerable & targeted browser by criminals. There is also a time delay in when the patch is released and the device is updated. Every day the vulnerability has existed that user, you, could be unknowingly infected with a virus; have your system used in an online attack, or your data from banks recorded and reused for ill-gotten gain.

Google Chrome updates itself automatically and more frequently when compared against Microsoft Internet Explorer. Internet Explorer tends to be more vulnerable to delay in applying patches due to the time between the release of the patch and when it is eventually adopted by the user computer.

To install Google's web browser "Chrome", simply navigate to the following link, and follow the instructions[9]:

- https://www.google.com/chrome/

---

8   Bromium Labs Research Brief EndPoint Exploitation Trends H1 2014

9   Chrome is recommended here for simplicity. While there are many very good browsers that exist beyond Chrome, the intent here is to avoid the shipped web browser with the operating system. Since Google has the smallest operating system market share in this text Chrome is recommended.

RULE OF THUMB

DEVICE	IDEAL WEB BROWSER
Microsoft Windows or Apple Computers	Google Chrome Mozilla Firefox Opera web brower
Apple iOS devices (tablets, smartphones)	Google Chrome Apple Safari Opera Mini web brower
Google Android devices (tablets, smartphones)	Mozilla Firefox Google Chrome Opera Mini web browser

#19 Using encryption is like wearing pants in public: it is better for everyone involved

On each web browser and site there is an option to encrypt your communication. This is incredibly important and valuable to you directly. In order to ensure you are using encryption look for the following indications in the website address bar:

- "https"
- a lock icon: 🔒 https:

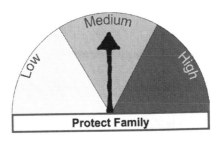

If you are doing anything online that you consider to be personal, private, or sensitive, be sure you are using encryption through this simple visual verification.

Encryption on a web browser is active when using "HTTPS". This technically means that your web browser is now using encryption to make it difficult to impossible for someone listening in the middle to see the transmitted data. Using encryption allows you to ensure that only your web browser and the store, bank, or website that is meant for the information can actually receive it. You can turn this on by simply typing "https://www...." Followed by your web address destination, and if the system supports encryption you will reach your desired website.

When I use websites for anything private or sensitive I verify that my browser is using HTTPS. If it is not, I try and update the address in the browser. This tip won't stop nation states from eavesdropping, but without encryption you and the emperor will be pant-less in public.

#20 When using a site...
and you finish - LOG OUT

Ever wonder why your bank's website automatically logs you out? Well, it is because they view your connection as trusted only while you are actively using the site. When you are done, they eliminate that access to protect you!

So, use the same logic on other sites such as social media sites and shopping sites.

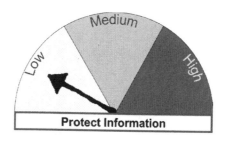

DEEPER INSPECTION OF IDEA:

So ... really, why should I log out?

When you fail to log out of a website the credentials (or token) remain on your computer and browser. As you navigate the web it remembers these credentials. If someone else uses your computer to access the web your computer and the websites you visit still THINK you are you and the one logged on, not your friend. Therefore all of the ads, automatically-filled fields, auto-logon and comment systems also think it's still you using the computer.

In addition, by remaining logged on you are inviting broader tracking and targeting of yourself online by advertisers, criminals, and predators.

PRIVACY ALERT – WHAT IS TRACKING?

Tracking – the use of identifiers given to you by websites

- Positive: These allow the sites to customize the appearance to your preferences
- Negative: Allows for collection of your behaviors; browsing history; see what you are viewing online; track your mouse placement on webpages; offer different pricing based on this collected information, and more

Think of this technology as a sticker. Everything you see and do on any site adds these stickers to your computer. So as you continue to browse the web, these accumulated stickers are available to see where and what you have been up to online.

"I can't tell if you are a 5 year old or an information security ninja"

#21 Challenge Questions: make up awesome **fictional** answers!

Develop a system for these questions by which you answer with atypical and inaccurate responses. For example, when asked for your birth city perhaps you elect to use a color as a response. This response would then be used any time you are asked by this business/web site, and therefore can easily be changed (without exposing your real personally identifiable information) to new responses for that single business/website.

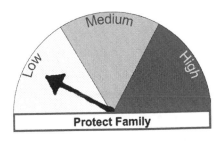

This system allows you to have unique responses and a higher level of security than celebrities and politicians.

DEEPER INSPECTION OF IDEA:

Most online systems make available a question and answer system to provide a way of regaining access to accounts when credentials are lost.

The responses that are sought by these Q&A systems are sometimes 'public' knowledge due to our ever connected lives, and therefore not very secure for the tasks at hand. In most cases the answers to these basic questions can be gained simply through public records, our Facebook/Social media profile, or a newspaper article.

Common challenge questions include:

- Where did you go to school?
- What was your first car?
- What is your mother's maiden name?

In a connected world these questions are terrible at stopping others from accessing your accounts, as they are easy to find through social media accounts or a quick Internet search.

To keep these safeguards effective make them personal, unique, fictional, and easy to remember! Easiest is to use a ledger either on paper stored at home, or through a password vault type software. (Highlighted in Chapter 9)

EXAMPLE PASSWORD LEDGER

NAME OF WEBSITE	USERNAME	PASSWORD	CHALLENGE & RESPONSE (TIP #21)
FINANCIAL SITES			
MESSAGING SITES			
SOCIAL MEDIA SITES			

Visit www.hntbh.com/free for a free printable version

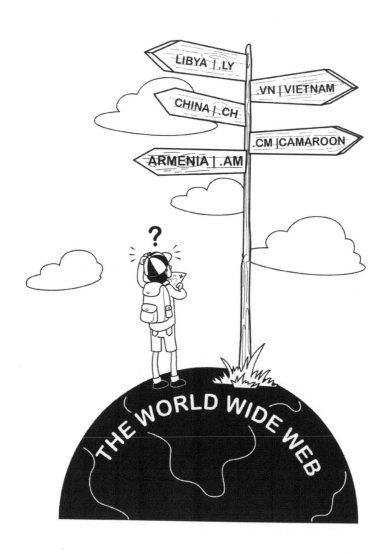

#22 Mind your geography by recognizing the most trusted regions

Every web address begins with an original name - Google, New York Times, etc. These are clear and obvious. Each address then ends with a period and either .com, .net. or .org. When seeking out these main business domains strongly consider those with the .COM, .NET, .ORG extensions. As the Internet has expanded and a need for more naming conventions has arisen, there are now over 1,000 new web extensions (web extensions = everything after the period). There are those that deal with types of businesses and one for each individual country.

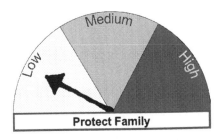

It is surprising how many people will fear traveling to a country due to physical harm, but have no idea they are sending their personal data to those regions. As an example, here are addresses that you may have used, but I have added the country name:

- YourCoffeeHouse.cm ⇨ YourCoffeeHouse.**Camaroon**
- NewsSite.ly ⇨NewSite.**Libya**

There are many fraudulent websites designed to harm you and infect your computer if you navigate to their website. Some bet on human error – many of these criminal sites operate on web extensions such as ".CO" and ".CM". These criminals are betting the user will forget one of the 3 letters of .COM and arrive at their website.

To identify a new site's web address use a search engine to find the proper full URL. Search engines will highlight whether is the link qualifies as an advertisement or if it is the authoritative source. Beware of sites that LOOK like the site, but are actually a competitor or third party trying to take advantage of the larger brand's reputation.

Stay in your geography (meaning try to navigate with businesses operating in your home country) if possible to maintain continuity of laws, privacy, and security 'general rules of thumb.'

CHAPTER 8

SOCIAL MEDIA

TIPS IN THIS CHAPTER:

- ✓ Identifying unsafe Friend & Followers
- ✓ Safeguarding social media credentials
- ✓ The benefit of adding verifications
- ✓ Being mindful when sharing and posting
- ✓ Stop geo-tagging to protect family and prevent thefts

Social media accounts are valuable to criminals for a few reasons – they provide personal details about you, they are excellent for spreading at scale malware to your connected 'friends', and typically provide indirect access to your other online accounts.

When a breach of an account happens the intruder is often not just after your data, which they are, but they are thinking bigger. By leveraging your account information from one social media account to hop to another system (i.e., they hijack your Facebook account and then try the same credentials for your twitter accounts; they then send messages to your trusted friends with malware designed to cause them financial and personal grief).

Many consider the online communities where we share and discuss everything from baby pictures to the latest news topics as personal spaces.

We connect and many of us have ongoing discussions with those we have met online only, only speaking on these platforms, and occasionally (less than 1 time every 2 years) see each other in person! As a result, these social platforms (Facebook, Twitter, LinkedIn, Instagram) are the source of truth and possess our very identities to our connections. Thus our connections trust what we share and say online. This relationship of trust of social media accounts is a target for criminals, bullies, and simply mean-spirited people.

It is up to us, as stewards of these online identities, to consistently ensure that we maintain control of our accounts and be mindful of what other's share to us.

6 Degrees of Separation – a game of finding the number of people it takes to make a connection to Kevin Bacon. This game is fun in the fact of realizing how few people it takes to connect, but also one can appreciate how many connections it really takes to reach that person. The distance of connections allows for confidence in communications and to some extent privacy.

In the world of LinkedIn and Facebook though it takes only 3 connections to reach anyone on Facebook[10]. That means most, if not all, things shared on Facebook can easily be seen by everyone, eventually. Social media is bringing together ideas, people, cultures, but also is a platform that is a target of criminals. Practicing the following tips will greatly reduce the impact of these criminals harming you, or your friends.

---

10   BBC Technology Article, Facebook users average 3.74 degrees of separation, November 23, 2011. URL

#23 Be wary of random "friend" & "follower" requests

When you receive an email or message from someone and it includes a link that you did not request even a friend request, you should NOT click on the link. This occurs in emails from services such as LinkedIn, Facebook, Twitter when you receive an official-looking message or request to connect.

As in any emailed link, do not click on those requests. Instead:
- go directly to the site in question
- view the request on the official site

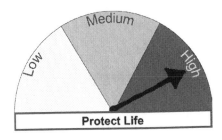

For requests from those with whom you are not familiar, vet the request objectively with the following considerations:
- How many mutual connections do you share?
- How personal and direct was the request?
- How "old" is the account making the request?
- How "active" has that account been over the last few months
- Is the account simply rebroadcasting (retweeting in twitter lingo), or is it sharing original with humanistic language?
- Contact a listed mutual friend, and verify their character directly

Phishing is a type of fraud which occurs when an attacker sends a target (you, in this case) a message that may sound very convincing (from a family member or your bank, and it may contain personal details). The message will contain a link and you naturally will want to click on it. Except now you know better, and as a result will not become a victim to this type of fraud.

#24 Do not logon onto any site with your social media account

A powerful tip shared in Chapter 9 is that we must never repeat the same password for any website or service. Similarly, we should not be reusing our social media accounts to logon onto other sites. While convenient to post a comment or setup a shopping account with these integrated solutions, it is best avoided.

The benefits of connecting only make sense when there is a direct advantage that you receive (note convenience is not an advantage that qualifies), such as linking your social media account to an analytics dashboard. Linking accounts together make sense if the sharing of data is for the betterment of you.

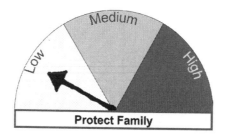

A BIT MORE DETAIL …

The social media and other online providers that make these "sign-in anywhere" feature do a good job securing your information. The grey area is the type and level of sharing of data between providers today and tomorrow. These change overtime as services evolve and the simplest approach is to not be caught having to keep up.

#25 Add secondary verification of identity to prevent account hijacks!

The widespread use and personal value of social networking sites and other community-based sites raises the value of these social sites. Therefore it is essential to add safeguards on each site that prevents account hijacking.

Verifications for identity are freely available on the following popular sites:

- Facebook:
    - » Login approvals
    - » SmartPhone identification
    - » Browser identification
- Twitter
    - » Phone verification
- Google
    - » Computer and device identification
    - » Two factor with tokens

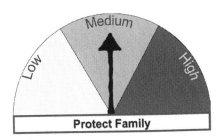

Each allows the use of a verification process (such as two factor authentication) when signing on or connecting the account. Turn this on by following the instructions on https://twofactorauth.org for the appropriate site.

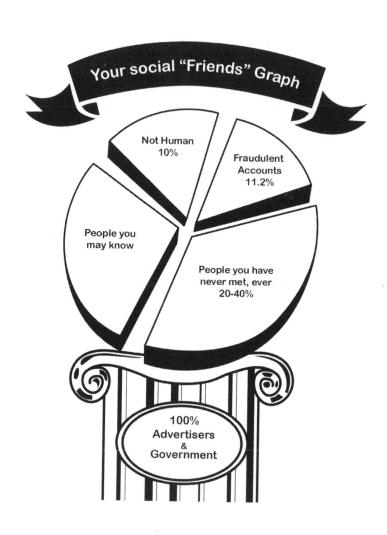

#26 Share your posts and photos with true friends, but not with the 'public'

Social media sites that allow you to connect to friends (such as Facebook, LinkedIn) provide you with options when you post a comment or photo so you can determine WHO can see it. Share posts and photos only with your connected friends.

Only post to the public when you are surveying for information or making a statement that excludes anything personal, financial, or any details about a trip.

Share your posts and photos with true friends, but not the 'public.' It is important to be aware of who are your 'friends' in this social network world. As the graphic highlights on the prior page, less than half of our 'friends' are actually those we really know. An interesting statistic in 2014 showed the following average number of friends[11]:

- 12 – 17 year olds: 521 "friends"
- 22 year olds: 1,000+ "friends"

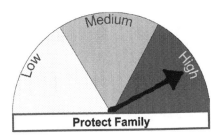

Also be sensitive to the reality that if you do not pay for a service (i.e., Facebook, SnapChat, etc...), then YOU are considered the product. To pay for the technology the details you share are available for sale to advertisers. This is how ads and the news feeds you see are populated and customized for you – using your shared posts!

---

11   Edison Research and Triton Digital, April 2014

#27 Disable geo-tagging on photos posted to public

When sharing photos and updates online using social media (such as Twitter, Facebook, Instagram) disable geo-tagging. This way if you wish to share to the world where you are at the moment you will be doing so intentionally.

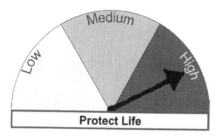

Also be aware that providing location data creates risks to not just you, but others. For instance, some criminals have used social media posts (about vacation) and geo-tagged photos online to rob people's homes and have house parties (true story!) while owners were away.

Photo Credit: Eleni de Wet

Geo-tagging is when your computer, mobile device, or phone adds the GPS coordinates of where you are to the picture data. This creates an opportunity for someone to rob you, impersonate you. An example for one of these schemes that is popular is where an impersonator sends family/friends a cry for help via e-mail or text messaging. The impersonator knows you are traveling due to the GPS tag, and uses the time zones to ask friends/family to send money ASAP. Typically the money request is due to an injury or event that makes it impossible for them to call you. Finally, geo-tagging could put at risk those you are visiting, such as the wildlife in Africa.

Technology and menus often change, so it is difficult to absolutely provide instruction on how to turn these off, but below are the current simple paths to disable geo-tagging:

- Apple / iOS (all devices)
    » Navigate to "Settings" > Privacy > Location Services
    » Turn off for all applications except those that you require it (such as a map or navigation application)
- Android devices:
    » Start camera application
    » Select the Settings button
    » Scroll down and find the GPS Tag option and turn it off

CHAPTER 9

SHARING AND PROTECTING YOUR PASSWORDS

TIPS IN THIS CHAPTER:

- ✓ Passwords as patterns
- ✓ How to stop memorizing passwords
- ✓ When to write passwords down & how to share
- ✓ Why you can text a password

In the beginning of the Internet (roughly 1977, though it was called a different name) there were no passwords. Anyone could access the computer system and networks. This lasted a few years but eventually led to a need for them ... why you might ask?

Passwords were added for a few specific reasons:

- System resources were impossible to balance and plan without a known potential user base
- Passwords created a mechanism to establish a payment model for computer time (in those days these computers were as rare as flights to space)
- Encouraged authenticity in the messages being received and to whom they were being delivered

Today is really no different except now we have many such credentials and they require good parenting. The best way to think of passwords is like keys on a key chain. Behaviors to consider:

- Would you leave your key in the lock at your house?
- Would you leave your house unlocked without any keys at all?
- Would you use the same key for your office, bike, home, and safe deposit box?

#28 To make a great password use a pattern!

Make sure your passwords are not easily guessable. Choose something that is not obviously tied to yourself (such as your birthdate) nor easily guessed by a computer, and therefore not discoverable to a criminal.

This can be done by creating a password based on a pattern that makes sense to you. Here are some examples of patterns that have proven successful:

- Use the web address for the site requiring a password and insert a number and extra symbols at a fixed point. An example would be:
  - » www.hntbh.com (this site's book portal)
  - » Password could be **www.hnt007!h.com**
- A keyboard pattern (i.e., you would press buttons to make a shape on the keyboard) plus the name of the site.
- Write a sentence within the password. This pattern requires you to remember the sentence and the number of letters of each word you'll use in the password, for example:
  - » Sentence: <u>Th</u>e <u>be</u>st <u>da</u>ys <u>are</u> <u>sp</u>ent <u>ru</u>nning <u>in</u> <u>th</u>e <u>mo</u>untains
  - » Password to use the first 2 letters: **"Thbedaarspruinthmo"**

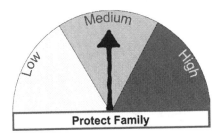

Protect Family

Never use the same password on more than 1 site

#29 How to juggle multiple passwords: use a wallet

In your wallet you carry your identification, credit cards, cash, coins, and a number of other important items. Each has its own place in the wallet and use in the world. Similarly, your username & password to access a website need such organization. You can manage them with a simple written journal, but if you ever stray from your home and need to log on this will not be sufficient. A digital wallet/vault for these passwords is the simplest solution.

The benefit here beyond convenience are these logs and password wallets ensure **we never use the same password for more than one site**!

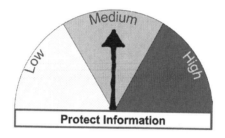

Purchasing a virtual "wallet" is a necessary expense. Please explore options that make sense for you. There are "wallets" available on the Apple App Store, at retailers, and available for download online. Choose a "wallet" that works for the devices you use to access sites which require passwords. The software wallets each have a demo/ free version to try and that would be the best first step. This will allow you time to try it out, confirm it works for you, and then you can purchase it directly.

A few good options include:

- **LastPass:** http://www.lastpass.com
- **1Password:** https://agilebits.com/onepassword
- **Dashlane:** https:// www.dashlane.com
- **PasswordSafe:** http://passwordsafe.sourceforge.net/

#30 Write down your passwords

You have passwords for your yoga class, child's lunch money, bank sites, retirement funds, and fantasy sports leagues -and those are just online. You also have a pile of passwords for your home internet modem, home router, wireless connection, and if you are ahead of the times, your Internet-connected thermostat and door locks. ALL of these need a good password and sometimes the simplest solution will work.

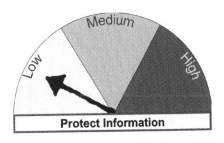

In this case – writing them down physically on paper works, but here are the ground rules for this cheat:

Passwords can be written down on paper for online sites. Examples include:

- Website passwords
- Smartphone in Application passwords
- Internet connected fitness-health gadgets
- Video game and streaming accounts

You can keep passwords for physical devices stored electronically, utilizing the password wallets highlighted in the prior Tip. Examples include:

- Internet modem
- Wi-Fi password
- Garage door codes

Note: in no circumstance should the password be kept WITH the item you are securing. i.e., you wouldn't tape the garage code to your garage door.

A DEEPER LOOK INTO THIS TIP

It is common for security professionals to advise against the writing down of passwords. This is for good reasons – these individuals are safeguarding devices that are in high traffic areas and the result of writing it down is more eyeballs gaining access. Think of a student getting into a teacher's desk to read a password off a notepad.

In our scenario we are focused on regular people and it is safe to write things down in our homes. The key is to store the password separately from the device in question. There it is safe to write down passwords for online websites. Nobody will physically be in your home to read the paper with the password for that website, and no hacker has the ability to "break" into that paper journal on your desk.

This is a tip to simplify your world with a low tech solution and should be done in conjunction with the other tips.

#31 Change passwords annually; like bathing it is necessary eventually

Despite our best efforts, problems happen with technology. People make mistakes and as a result the credentials you use may become less secret than when you first entered them into a website. All passwords need to be updated annually. This will greatly limit the damage caused by a criminal breach and help prevent loss of your data.

In most cases a breach will occur months before a business identifies the event, and it may be a few more months before law enforcement finishes investigating the breach. Therefore, changing your passwords is a good preventative measure to take in our connected world.

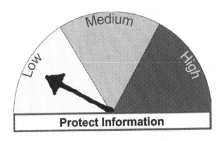

METHODS

Change every password at the same every year. This should NOT occur during tax season or during a time when you are about to travel, as these are historically the worst times (stressful and critical times when everything is running smoothly is not the time to reset account settings).

- Use that handy printout / journal of your passwords that you manage and check off each one as you modify it!
- When changing the password you need only to modify one character, so perhaps you add a number, or a symbol
- If you are using a password wallet as recommended, updates can be automated
- Clean house – delete unused services, forever

#32 Yes, share your passwords if you must... BUT change them within 24 hours

There will always be situations in which someone else needs to use your username and password. If the person is someone you trust then there is no reason not to share these credentials.

When you do share, however, you must change that password within 24 hours or sooner. There are simply too many variables at play here which can cause harm if you delay.

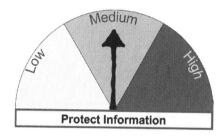

Remember: it is not the person borrowing the password who we distrust, but the computing systems involved in the process. We simply don't know the other person's security settings, anti-virus, etc. So it's best to change the password quickly after it has served the needed purpose to eliminate the risk!

#33 Tell your family and friends your mobile phone PIN

The unlock PIN on your phone is designed to prevent unauthorized persons from stealing your device reselling the hardware, installing malicious software, or simply causing you embarrassment. On most new mobile phones, a PIN ensures that a criminal cannot access your phone's data. This protects your contact lists, email, saved personal information, and files from being used to harm you or those you love.

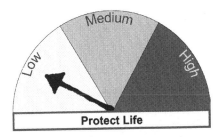

Our friends and family are the people who will be around to call 911, the doctor's office, or your daughter's school in case of an emergency. some mobile phones (tablets also benefit from this Tip), may have a pattern instead of a pin;, those should be shared similarly too.

So SHARE that PIN.

#34 If you are sharing a password, use your phone to send it in a text message!

If you share your Amazon, social media, bank, or emergency helicopter rescue account service username and password which are used to access an Internet site you are at risk of the password being captured and used in an online attack by a criminal.

The simplest solution is avoid sharing the credentials on the Internet and instead pass them along either in person, over the phone, via text message, or by SOME OTHER METHOD (carrier pigeons are absolutely viable though high maintenance).

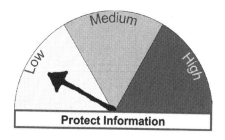

RULE OF THUMB:

- If the account information is for an Internet service, share it off the Internet

DEEPER INSPECTION OF IDEA

The brilliance of computers is they are masters of doing repeatable tasks efficiently and without delay. Criminals often set up computers to scan for usernames and passwords for specific sites on computers that have been hacked (without the user's knowledge, of course), or listen on hacked servers which are passing the data around.

If we share specific user credentials to online sites these computers can read that information and then instantaneously use it to access those sites. They may simply access your account or they may download specific data credentials and use it to send spam, or add a piece of software that will cause you harm in the future.

Bottom line: sharing data in a digital area where it can be automatically captured and used is against our pursuit of reducing / eliminating harm.

Another example: Emailing your username and password to someone is a terrible idea. Even sending the username and password in separate emails is a terrible idea. If a criminal has access to your email, both emails will be reliably sent to the criminal in an immediate fashion.

CHAPTER 10

WHILE YOU TRAVEL

TIPS IN THIS CHAPTER:

✓ Why and when to lock computer
✓ Prevent accidental harm with Sync features
✓ Setting a good PIN
✓ Prevent sharing data via Wi-Fi / Bluetooth
✓ Safety and protection from theft

Traveling is something I do quite a lot. On average I travel 225,000 miles a year by plane. It has exposed me to worlds and cultures that are so different it is impossible to easily communicate it to my family. One thing that I have learned though is that with the different cultures, laws, and histories come a significant need to behave differently.

We all hear about respecting cultures and knowing their social norms. But I want to stress that the mere fact you are away from home requires a different behavior; you simply must be more aware of your surroundings.

The tips here highlight behaviors to limit the physical loss of items and the risks that are increased because of the digital technology you are carrying – specifically your mobile phone, tablet, computer, fitness tracker, etc.

Each of these devices need to be backed up and its settings adjusted while you are traveling. This will make them slightly less simple and fun to use, but it is only temporary. The result is you'll have less theft, lower replacement costs, and almost zero loss of your electronic information.

Be present when traveling, and be mindful of your surroundings. this will ensure a wonderful trip, every time.

QUICK PRE-TRIP CHECK LIST

1. **Photocopy** – Identification, credit cards (front & back), and share with a friend who is not traveling with you.
2. **Empty** – Wallet and purse of non-essential cards and personal identification
3. **Backup** – Phone, tablet, and computer to an external drive or online service (Tip #41)
4. **Disable** – Wi-Fi auto-join and Bluetooth discovery from devices for trip (Tips #38, 39)
5. **Limit** – Social Media sharing to personal friends and turn off Geo-tagging for all public (i.e., Twitter, Instagram) posts (Tips #26, 27)
6. **Email** – your itinerary and important contact phone numbers to yourself

#35 When leaving your laptop or tablet on your seat to 'stretch', lock it!

When traveling it is convenient to bring along a device on which you can read, play on the internet, or simply bang out some e-mails. The only caveat is to be sure you lock your computer or device if you leave it sitting on your seat unattended.

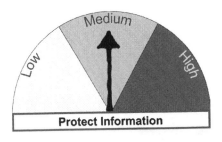

By lock, I mean you should engage the software screensaver/lock screen. No, it is not necessary to tie it to the seat or do anything more extreme.

Locking the screen safeguards all of your data and protects you from prying eyes. You never know who may be associated with you, your customer, or something you are writing on your computer.

Keep it simple and safe: lock it.

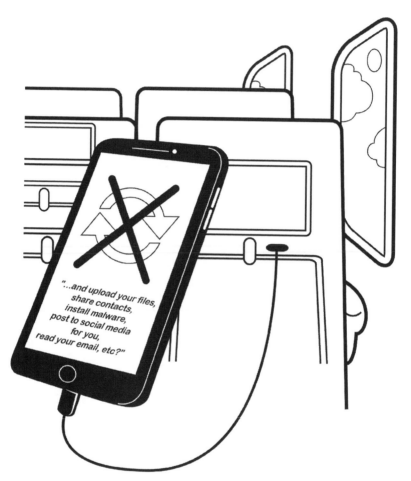

"Do you want to sync/trust this system...?"

#36 When connecting your mobile device to a foreign car or plane, Do Not Sync

There are marvelous places to plug in your mobile device's USB cable to recharge, to play music, etc... These are very useful when you are traveling, but you should adopt the following practice:

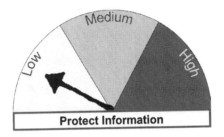

Connect only for power. On 'iOS devices' lock your phone first and then connect. The phone will prompt you for a confirmation to "trust" the connection. The answer is NO. This will allow your device to charge, but it will not allow the car/plane/connection to download or upload content to your device.

#37 Turn ON a security PIN
for your mobile device

While you should always have a security PIN on your mobile device to prevent criminals from accessing your data, when you travel it is especially important due to the higher potential for theft/loss of the device.

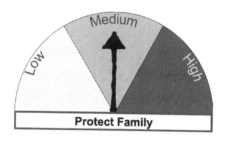

In most cases having a PIN allows your device to encrypt and protect your sensitive data from others. It also means that your personal information - accounts, emails, contacts, notes, videos, photos, and social media accounts - will all be safeguarded from attackers.

The PIN[12] should be something easily remembered and known by your traveling companions. But it should NOT be one of the following:

- 1234
- 0000
- 2580
- 1111
- 5555
- 5683
- 0852
- 2222
- 1212
- 1998

---

12   SplashData 2014 annual list of <u>worst passwords</u>

MOST COMMONLY USED PASSWORDS

- "123456"
- "password"
- "12345"
- "12345678"
- "qwerty"
- "abc123"

PASSWORDS THAT ARE EASILY GUESSABLE

- Your birthdate
- Your birth year
- Your wedding date
- Your child's birthday
- Graduation year
- Your favorite sports team

#38 Turn off - 'auto join Wi-Fi networks'

Mobile devices (smartphones, tablets) generally prefer to be connected to the internet via Wi-Fi. This typically allows them to operate at faster speeds, and is often cheaper for the user (free Wi-Fi vs. cellular data plans).

When you are traveling, however, engaging the "auto join" setting tells your mobile device constantly to broadcast itself and try to connect to any/all available wireless connections. For example, if an attacker has set up a wireless access point your smartphone will connect and share your personal device details. The attacker can then track your phone and even access your contacts' information.

This is dangerous and is essentially the same as shaking hands with every (yes EVERY) person you pass on the street. At some point your instincts may tell you to hesitate, but your phone will not hesitate.

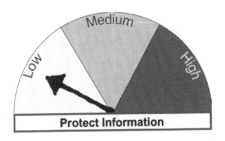

DEEPER INSPECTION OF IDEA

The easiest solution is simply to adjust your device's settings so it will NOT auto-join networks. This safeguard can be employed all the time or turned on only when traveling. I keep it engaged all the time–and join just the networks that I know and trust. This way my device connects only with networks I have confirmed, and it requires very little effort as my device remembers the networks to which I have previously connected.

This method is not perfect and works best when one is in familiar areas. When I travel abroad, I always turn off Wi-Fi and only turn it on when I know precisely which Wi-Fi network I am connecting to at the establishment.

#39 Turn off Bluetooth

Smartphones have the ability to allow short range wireless accessories such as wireless speakers and ear pieces to pair with them. This technology allows short range communication, but leaving it active, is risky and wastes battery power.

When traveling and not using such an accessory, simply turn off your Bluetooth connectivity. This is a very easy action on Android and Apple devices. This will prevent hacks from happening and ensure you have more battery life. If you have paired devices and must have Bluetooth active when traveling, simply set it to "Allow only to be visible to paired devices".

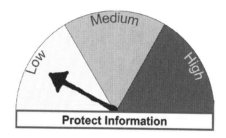

DEEPER INSPECTION OF IDEA

Attackers have found ways to remotely access a phone (when within range) and use it to make calls, access data, listen to conversations and use your data connection to use the internet. This compromises your personal information and privacy as well as your family and friends' contact details. The Bluetooth signal - think of it as a "radio", just like the Wi-Fi "radio" - signal is constantly broadcast in an effort to connect with other "radios". Like anything else, there are good radios and bad radios.

It has been proven that Bluetooth is a good attack approach for criminals whose targets are on trains, in stadiums, in bars, and of course, in coffee shops[13].

---

13   Bluetooth attack to piggyback for long distance charges, Wired; Kaspersky research on attacks, 2015

#40 Change the background image of device to show RETURN to me info

We sometimes misplace our phones at friends' houses, in cabs, and at restaurants. To recover these devices we end up retracing our steps physically, or try to call the device in the hopes that someone will answer and inform us of its location.

Instead, make a background image that includes an alternate contact phone number / name (this phone and name should be a real person). This way if your device is found at the airline counter or in a cab the kind soul is able to use that information to contact you and return the device.

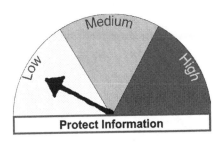

DEEPER INSPECTION OF IDEA

The idea is to change your background image, or "locked screen" image, when traveling. The info to include is simply:

- An alternate phone number
- A name

This image can be made easily with an App, or most simply done by writing the details on a piece of paper; taking a picture, and then making it your wallpaper for the trip. The upside is this can be easily swapped in while traveling and then your background returned to fun family photos when you return from your travels.

#41 Backup your device before going on trip

When preparing to leave on a trip be sure to plug in your mobile device or initiate a wireless backup (if setup on the device) and confirm you have a complete back up of your data before departing. If you will be traveling with the computer that you used to back up your mobile device be sure to have additionally backed up the data on the computer once you've finished with the mobile device.

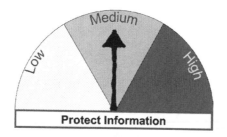

KEY STEPS:

- The night before traveling, plug in your mobile device (phone, tablet) and allow the data to be backed up and synced.
- Overnight, have your computer backed up to an external hard drive.
- In the morning, take both devices and have an awesome trip!

Think of it as the best insurance ever: all your thoughts, pictures, and settings can be brought back to the exact moment before you left for your trip. The purpose of backing up your device before the trip is to provide protection and a path to recovering your pictures, papers, and music should you lose or damage your device on the trip!

#42 Place electronics in the trunk before arriving in a sketchy area!

When driving your own car or a rental in a foreign country, city, town, or gas station the best place to store electronics (such as tablets, computers) is out of sight. The trunk of your vehicle is a great place to stash these items.

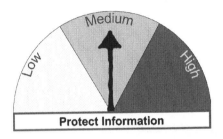

The most effective way to use this tip includes adopting the following habits:

- Place devices in trunk before you begin travel
- Keep devices in trunk when at gas station, hotel parking lot, restaurant
- If you think you may be in an unknown area when you stop for gas, put devices in the trunk when you depart so they are out of sight before you arrive
- Trunks tend to be messy (I am sure yours is not), so they take a long time to sift through. An extra ten seconds of effort on your part can be very effective in thwarting a theft
- If you are parking overnight put your iPhone/android charging cables out of site so a potential thief doesn't have an extra reason to check your car for electronics

CHAPTER 11

HOW TO PROTECT YOUR LAPTOP AT SCHOOL AND WORK

TIPS IN THIS CHAPTER:
- ✓ Physical and digital locks
- ✓ Timing backups to save your memories
- ✓ Browser password storage

Physical theft of technology occurs and when it does is a very personal violation m. Most thefts don't occur when we travel abroad, but based on studies over 50% from office/workplace and a laptop is stolen every 53 seconds[14]. Smartphones suffer equally from these physical thefts and according to another survey, victims would be willing to pay up to $1,000 to recover the device (this amount is based on the sentimental value and not market value of the device[15]) . This means there is certainly a higher probability for us having an accident or being a victim to such theft. Thankfully there are a few things you can do to reduce the pain of these events.

I categorize the loss of a device by the emotion and value of the ideas and mementoes in the device and less about the physical cost of replacement. Especially since in most cases insurance covers the

---

14   Gartner Research, Ponemon Institute and Dell report

15   IDG Research report on behalf of Lookout, 2014

replacement cost. The loss of such personal information is akin to a fire in your home. Nobody cares about the house (it is inconvenient), but everyone grieves of the loss of pictures.

This is about preserving your ideas, pictures, contact information, and that which cannot be replaced with money but was built with time and love.

#43 If you are in an apartment or open work space, lock it down

It's very simple. Most laptops likely have slots that allow you to connect the laptop directly to a security cable. These are relatively cheap (around $50) and are easy to use with either a key or a passcode. They can be used to secure the computer/device to a piece of furniture and are especially useful when working in temporary spaces. There are key and numerical keypad versions. Either type is sufficient.

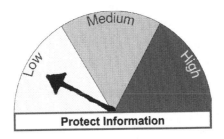

#44 Backups are important, but physically separate the backup from the device

Backing up your data is necessary because both humans and hardware can fail. If you experience a loss involving your main computer, having a backup can return your ideas to you as they were written. This is peace of mind that an insurance policy simply cannot offer.

The back-up device needs to be stored separately and away from the space where your computer rests. Here are a few rules of thumb to follow when backing up your data:

- At school, your backup device should be a secure online backup service
- Your work computer should be backed up at home (as permitted) or using a work-provided method
- Never store your backup device with the main computer because failing to keep them separate means they are susceptible to the same threat of a criminal event or natural disaster

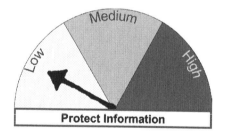

WHAT NOT TO DO:

- Store the backup drive in your laptop bag
- Keep the backup device next to the school laptop when not needed

#45 When away, lock the screen

It's a simple, yet extremely important habit. Whenever you step away from your computer in a public space, at school, or in an office setting you should always activate the lock the screen function. This can be done through the following simple methods:

- Microsoft products
  - » Enter at the same time: "Windows key + L", or
  - » Setup screensaver to require a password to unlock
- Apple products:
  - » Computers, navigate to: System Preferences > Security & Privacy > General
  - » Turn on "hot corners" to enable easily with the swipe of your finger

Be sure a passcode will be required for anyone to log on. Your work will remain safe if you take advantage of the security methods that already exist on your computer.

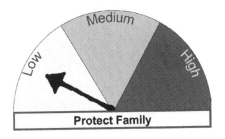

DEEPER INSPECTION OF IDEAS

Locking the screen means a password will be needed to return to the same session. This means all of your work, web browsing, and social activities are safe from the eyes of others. This also protects the device if it is stolen, as the criminal will have to get past the security feature in order to access your data. This is more effective if you have turned on the "require password at boot" setting. Be sure to do that, too!

#46 Require a password for system startup

All systems allow you to set up a username and password which can be required to start a computer (commonly referred to as the bios password) or after it is booted you can require a logon to access the computer files. You should engage this feature as it provides a specific safeguard for your privacy and, in the event the machine is stolen, the data will be significantly harder to access.

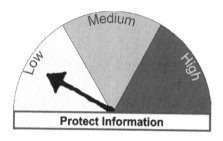

DEEPER INSPECTION OF IDEA

When a system is fraudulently accessed, it is often because the system was left unattended and unlocked.. Another possible scenario involves the theft of the computer itself. If a password is required, the data is significantly more secure from prying eyes and a criminal will not be able to gain access when the system is restarted.

Do not become lazy and turn on 'auto-login' features, as this would negate everything you have done to secure your data and protect your privacy.

#47 Disable your web browser from remembering passwords

If you share a computer with a roommate, coworkers, or others, do not store your passwords in the web browsers. Most browsers allow you to view all saved passwords instantly in plain text if you have the password to the computer. All of the passwords for web browsers are available in a menu with each browser, and the asterisks you see on web pages are not present. These could easily be printed or saved to a document. If your office has shared computers everyone already has access to the password required to log on.

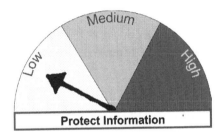

SOLUTIONS

Web browsers give you the ability to save passwords on your computer. On some web browsers you can even save the passwords onto the Internet, and any web browser that you are logged into can access those passwords. For example: if your home computer has saved passwords and you log onto services such as Google email, the web browser can synchronize the passwords from both computers to each browser. In this scenario the only things protecting your banking, personal thoughts, social media accounts, and privacy is the character of those using that computer and their careful attention to avoid accidentally installing a virus or malware.

Disabling the saved password setting or simply choosing not to save a password in your web browser is all you must do to prevent others from accessing your passwords on a shared computer.

OTHER OPTIONS:

- Setup a password vault/wallet software to store the passwords This is the simplest option
- Setup a unique user ID on the computer, but this requires everyone to log onto a system to use it and suspend other user sessions – not always easy for everyone involved

CHAPTER 12
HOW TO PARENT IN AN ONLINE AGE

TIPS IN THIS CHAPTER:
- ✓ Approving and knowing 'Friends'
- ✓ Deny geo-tagging and thwart predators
- ✓ No kid safe Internet exists

For social media to work, every image, video, sound, and text that is produced is copied, saved, or published at least 30 times to exist on the site on which you intended it to exist. As parents it is your responsibility to educate, interact, police, correct, and control the online experience. This is much like crossing parking lots to get to the store. As the little one progresses from carrier to walking while holding hands to staying 'by your side', so should they progress in these online systems.

Of course, it is quite difficult to keep up with technology, so we will have to stay engaged and maintain that good communication so sought for throughout their development. Beyond the truth that the information shared is highly likely to be seen forever by anyone motivated to see it – it is also important to recognize that criminals and creepy individuals work these digital streets.

While I was writing this book, one individual contacted me on www.facebook.com/hntbh. Someone hacked her smartphone and used it to take pictures of his/her children. Parents must be vigilant across all devices.

#48 Control the Friending function

If your children are old enough to use social networks and have their own gadgets then you need to know their friends and contacts. This means you must review all of their "Friends." Yes, every one of them.

This will ensure that your children are not subject to viewing illicit content, are not being approached by criminals (beyond "just" the hackers), and are not falling victim to blind cyberbullying.

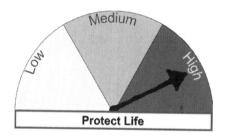

IT IS NOT EASY …

To accomplish this daunting task each parent must adopt a sustainable method. Start by openly discussing this rule of review with your children: they must agree to give you full access to THEIR accounts. You will not simply use your social network account to review their activity, but instead you will log into their accounts to review their relationships and activity. As your children get older you can rely on your own external view if you wish, but you need to be sure you are aware of all activity.

Having full access to the account allows you to change the security and privacy settings as appropriate over time. social media companies frequently revise their privacy policies; it is up to you to update settings as necessary.

The rule of thumb is "Friends" are known persons who you could call on the telephone and all others go in "other", which is where more generalized posts and online connections can be set up. This will simplify posting and allow for the customization of how sharing occurs; In other words you control what your children share online.

#49 Disable geo-tagging

Turn off geo-tagging on your children's mobile devices and remove geo-tagging from their online activities. This will only be semi-effective, as other Friends often reveal their location in their posts and state you were with them.

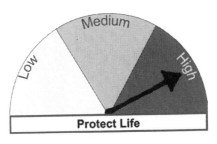

Geo-tagging occurs when GPS coordinates are added to a post or photo. This is very convenient when trying to coordinate with friends at a concert or while traveling, but care must be taken, as revealing location information can leave your children vulnerable to stalkers, bullies, and predators (82% of online sex crimes against minors used victim's likes & dislikes, and 65% used social media sites to gain home and school information).

Some social media services have removed your ability to Geo-tag photos and posts. Twitter has taken this position, but this can be overridden by the user. The opposite is true for other social media services, and a few that make geo-tagging a product benefit. Being mindful about geo-tagging will increase each person's personal safety.

#50 For anyone under 16, don't reveal last names online

Actual friends can easily find us online, and those who cannot find us probably shouldn't! As individuals get older it is 'OK' to use last names. This is because so much information about us is available online by the time we reach adulthood that the decision is essentially out of our hands.

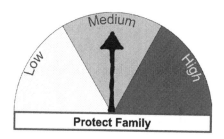

Privacy of personal information and your ability to limit the public availability (despite that being the point of many of these social networks) of the shared information should be your goal. If this can be achieved, then the identity and safety of the underage individual can be maintained for a longer period.

#51 Illicit content is on all platforms; monitor and parent what is appropriate

There is no technology or setting that will safeguard children from all illicit online content. Being successful in this endeavor requires time, effort, and parent engagement. Considering the speed with which technology changes, it is not reasonable to assume a 100% solution will exist anytime soon.

You must teach your children what content is appropriate and personally monitor their usage of devices. This includes everything from Kindle books to Google Docs, YouTube, and even online games. The best practice is to have your children use these electronic devices in your presence. Proximity is an excellent social tool and generally enough to limit exposure to illicit content, as the parent can immediately correct actions and the child learns right/wrong very quickly.

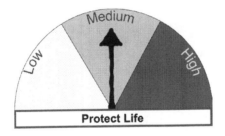

UNFORTUNATELY ...

Social platforms and electronic Internet connected systems are not designed for children and while many businesses set up children protected zones, these are not perfect. Content can slip through the cracks and be quickly copied and shared. Sometimes criminals even execute pranks aimed at pushing inappropriate content to these protected zones for children.

Again, no silver bullets here - just good old-fashioned parenting.

CHAPTER 13
RECOVERING FROM A HACK

TIPS IN THIS CHAPTER:

- ✓ Data breach todo list
- ✓ When to replace credit cards and account info
- ✓ Locking credit files for family
- ✓ Unwinding medical identity fraud
- ✓ Protecting gaming characters

The preceding chapters have identified behaviors that reduce the probability of your personal information being exposed to criminals as well as the impact of an information data breach should one occur. The remaining sections of this book assume that a breach has occurred and focus on how you should respond to the breach.

The tips in this chapter and the next explain the first actions you should take based on current trends in criminal exploitation of stolen information. This certainly doesn't replace specific law enforcement procedures or customized solutions from an expert service that specializes in recovering such information.

The following details describe the behaviors you will need to adopt in order to protect and fortify yourself, and to reduce the likelihood you will suffer additional harm as the result of a breach. To help you prioritize your actions I have researched and developed the following table to assist you. Tips appear along the top axis and on the left axis you will find the type of data that can be revealed in the event of a hack. To use this table effectively, find the type of data that was exposed by the breach and then focus on following the listed tips immediately.

All of the tips I have shared within this book are powerful and are most effective when done together, but time is finite and I appreciate the need to identify the most critical next steps should disaster strike. To support that preservation of time and focus on the key activities, the following table provides a guide.

	Replace Credit Card	Credit Report (personal)	Business Report	Lock / Freeze Credit	Offline Medical File	Financial Password Reset	Monitoring & Preventive Svc	Open new bank accounts	Refresh Online Accounts
Names			■						
Dates of birth			■		■				
Social Security numbers		■	■	■	■	■	■		
Health care information	■				■		■		
Email addresses									■
Employment Information		■							
Bank Account		■	■	■			■	■	
Credit Card	■		■						
Challenge & Response questions				■			■		■
Passwords						■			■

#52 Call and report lost
credit card immediately

The simplest way to eliminate the hassle and damage of a criminal breach of your credit card information is to request the card provider to send you a new card. It is such an easy process that I change my credit cards at least once per year!

The process is simple. Call the phone number listed on the back of your card and state that you need a replacement card. If you are asked why you need a new card you can refer to the breach or simply explain that it was lost.

This ensures that ANYONE attempting to use your old credit card number will be denied, instantly protecting you from any potential future damage.

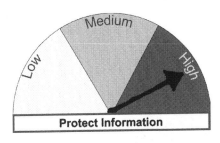

MORE GOOD NEWS...

An extra benefit of canceling a credit card is that any subscriptions and/or recurring billing payments connected to the account will be halted. This forced me to reconsider whether the monthly services for which I was being billed were worth the expense. The cleanse was great for my financial hygiene and saved me over $1,000 per year! Those $5 and $10 per month service fees can add up very quickly.

#53 Never submit your username or password to a website to 'check' if it was breached

When a data breach occurs and the topic hits the news media someone (perhaps a criminal) will typically set up a website that offers to check your credentials to determine whether or not they were part of the breached data set. This is just a ruse to get you to share your credentials and personal information.

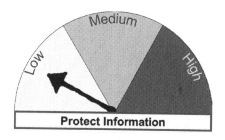

Don't fall for this trick. Never enter your personal information or log on information onto a site for such a purpose. If a company/website you frequent experiences a breach, the company will ask you only to reset it and will NOT request that you type your credentials for verification.

Simple rule of thumb: instead of checking through a third party website, just change your password!

#54 Request a copy of your credit report from all 3 credit bureaus

These reports provide a snapshot of your personal current financial state for all open accounts, requested credit applications, outstanding loans, and more. The first time you receive these reports immediately confirm that all of the listed facts and accounts are correct. It is very easy to make corrections if you find errors, so do it.

Verify that the reports remain correct perhaps six months or a year later. You can compare each new report to the older ones and ensure you alone are responsible for the activity on your reports. If information breached included tax information or that of your children or spouse a similar credit report should be sought for them too.

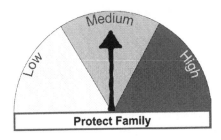

USEFUL LINKS:
- Centralized credit report request site:
  - » https://www.annualcreditreport.com
- Links to the 3 major credit bureaus:
  - » equifax.com
  - » experian.com
  - » transunion.com

#55 Regular business credit report reviews to stop illegal credit lines

Pull a business credit report for your personal business to prevent hijacking of credit lines. This should be done at least every six months or once each year, and then consistently every 12 months if no fraudulent activity appears. This is especially prudent if your personal business relies on your own personal credentials, identification, and authority to transfer funds or open additional lines of credit. The details you should search for include:

- In-depth credit history
- Banking, insurance and leasing information
- Bankruptcy filings
- Judgment filings against your business
- Tax lien filings levied against your business
- Credit inquiries made in the last nine months on behalf of your business

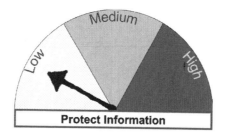

In addition to the previously mentioned credit bureaus, the firm Dunn and Bradstreet (www.dnb.com) provides additional service reports.

#56 Request a lock on your personal credit file and those of your family members

This is a classic defense and one of the simplest and perhaps most effective methods of protecting your credit. It can be done for both adults and children with no risk of harming one's financial future. This is a low cost and significantly more effective action than other methods. It is actively defensive (meaning it will prevent and inhibit criminals from harming you) rather than a detective control. A detective control would be a service that sends you notice of suspected activity – this is helpful, but far more burdensome.

Credit files are maintained at three bureaus in the United States, so you must lock your credit at each individual bureau. You should do this for each of your family members as noted in the provided table of tips and actions. While not every credit application requires a credit check, the big ones – like buying a house, car, or boat - will be covered.

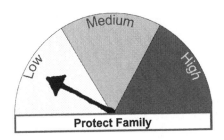

This can complicate making large purchases that require a credit approval. If a lock is in place, the credit check will come back as an error, because the system is being rejected. A temporary unlock is required when making such transactions, and instructions should be saved to your phone or wallet for future reference.

USEFUL LINKS

- Equifax: https://www.freeze.equifax.com
- Experian: https://www.experian.com/consumer/cac/InvalidateSession.do?code=FREEZE
- TransUnion: http://www.transunion.com/personal-credit/credit-disputes/credit-freezes.page

#57 Create a personal copy
of medical facts to protect against
Medical Identity Theft

Request copies of your past medical procedures, medications, allergies, and scans from your medical providers. The federal law known as HIPAA mandates the sharing of such information. Furthermore, the information must be provided to the patient at a reasonable cost. Many states have established specific dollar limits for these costs.

Use your medical records to maintain the integrity of your medical history, which may be depended upon for future treatment. this also provides a method of monitoring what medical procedures have been submitted to your insurance company and may help you spot any fraudulent activity.

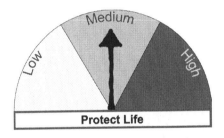

Note that the criminal modification of health information is a serious problem and could create a life-threatening situation should information regarding a patient's allergies be modified.

TASKS:
- Contact your primary care doctor and obtain a full copy of your file
- Document procedures, surgeries, and medications
- Request all claims and identification information from insurance company

- Ask insurance company about available security and file integrity options
- Verify that medical and allergy information is matched to insurance records
- Review all claims annually to identify any criminal activity.

#58 Refresh financial accounts with new passwords and Two-Factor verification

Financial accounts include those of your checking and savings provider. In addition, this must include mortgage, car loan, government tax site, retirement account, and other such accounts. Take special care to know all of the sites that you depend on protecting your data – especially those you infrequently use. It is common when a new account is opened, or as an update to old accounts that online access is enabled.

This is another way to prevent your money from being stolen electronically. People often overlook this step because they assume their financial institutions are inherently secure, but we must remember that these institutions are no more secure than any other website or online service. We lock our car doors. We should be just as vigilant in safeguarding our online information. After a potential data break at a financial institution - such as a story on the news or a letter/email stating your data may have been exposed – you should operate *as if your data has been compromised.* You must change your credentials used to log on to the service provider's site.

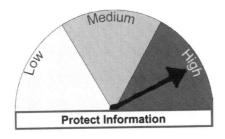

ACTIONS:
- Update online passwords
- Add token or phone verification pin for logging on to site
- Add token or phone verification PIN for transfers of any money

#59 Add credit monitoring & preventive services for all members in your household

Add credit monitoring and preventive services for you and your family members, including your six-year-old daughter. These services are more passive and have an associated fee, but are designed to be real-time and adapt to criminals' evolving activities. Basic credit monitoring services (commonly offered after a data breach, but these services will not prevent or protect your family from the current threats. More beneficial proactive services are available.

These services cannot replace the tips offered within this book, as the tips ensure that your information is not reused and is protected for a lifetime. One service that provides a greater level of sophistication and a wider scope of protection is CoreID. Think of it as a concierge service used to protect your identity. CoreID handles everything from detecting the breach to filing of police reports and orchestrating the clean-up process.

While most think of their personal identity as their physical presence and things they can touch – their home, car, or other belongings identities today online hold equal footing with these physical identities. In other words, your online professional and personal reputation is immensely important. For some this reputation is worth as much as credit bureau FICO scores and real dollars in the bank. Several effective services are available. and Reputation Defender is one that I am familiar with and recommend.

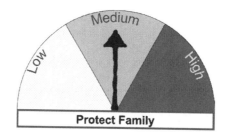

OPTIONS:

- Credit Agency fraud monitoring service (Equifax, Experian, TransUnion)
- Equifax: https://www.equifax.com
- Experian: https://www.experian.com/
- TransUnion: https://www.transunion.com
- Active fraud prevention and detection (CoreID) concierge services
  » www.coreidservices.com
- Online reputation management and clean-up (Reputation Defender)
  » www.reputation.com

Core ID Services 20% discount code for How Not To Be Hacked readers: HNTBH

Reputation.com discount link for How Not To Be Hacked readers: https://me.reputation.com/hntbh

---

SPECIAL BONUS

Gain access to unpublished tips, news articles, all book references, and updates as they happen!

Simply send me an email: Tips@hntbh.com
Or visit online: www.hntbh.com/free

#60 Replace accounts that were exposed in a crime or breach

To prevent another theft once you have recovered funds and regained your footing, you should close any bank accounts exposed or at risk and obtain new account numbers.

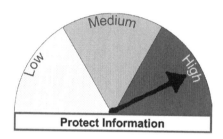

Similar to when a credit card is lost or stolen (physically or from a data breach at a retailer) you will get a new card number and a new bank account number This is especially important for savings accounts, checking accounts, and other accounts from which you can write checks or transfer money.

Work with your bank to coordinate the recovery of funds and then the full closure and opening of a new, separate account. Remember that the intent is to stop future problems, so verify that the old account is closed and the new account is independent of the others.

It is important to be aware of any auto-withdrawals (such as a mortgage or car payment) associated with these accounts, as you will need to update your account information with these businesses.

#61 Refresh online & gaming accounts to prevent loss of data and 'characters'

Now is the time to log onto your favorite online and gaming sites to refresh the passwords. An online account is any site that hosts your files. For each account, consider adding a phone number for verification when changes are made to your account. Facebook and other sites offer different anti-account hijacking safeguards, at no cost.

The use of these online accounts is so pervasive we often forget how much we depend up on them. On average a person spends ~4 hours a day on these sites, which is more time than we reserve for EATING!

Gaming accounts are also important to safeguard due to the time investment and identity associated with these accounts. Be sure to refresh your passwords associated with these accounts, especially as some of these game accounts have expanded to become more than just systems for gaming For example, Xbox now uses Hotmail.

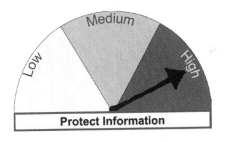

ACCOUNTS TO MONITOR/SAFEGUARD:
- Xbox Account
- Sony PlayStation Account
- Facebook
- Apple iTunes
- Amazon
- Google Account / Play
- Yahoo Accounts (and partner sites)

#62 Remove embarrassing digital files

Storing any SENSITIVE or EMBARRASSING files online? Now is a great time to erase them and follow the previously shared tips on refreshing the passwords and two factor authentication. Common places where such publicly embarrassing emails, pictures, and videos may be found include: your private YouTube channel, an Apple iCloud drive, or an online file sharing site such as DropBox.

Change your passwords frequently and consider removing the potentially embarrassing files altogether. Better safe than famous.

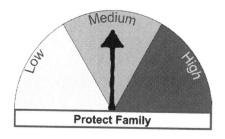

SITES TO CHECK FOR EMBARRASSING FILES:
- YouTube (Personal)
- YouTube (Professional)
- Facebook Fan Page
- Apple iCloud
- DropBox
- Amazon Cloud Services
- Google App

CHAPTER 14

HOW TO ADAPT TO THE FUTURE

IN THIS CHAPTER:
- ✓ Post identity theft success factors
- ✓ Future proofing the tips to each new gadget
- ✓ Bonus tip ... free credit reports all year

This book provides a foundation of information to limit the probability of a breach occurring and the impact any such breach would have on you and your family. Adopting these behaviors will put you on the same level as the smartest and most tech savvy individuals in their fields. The previous chapter discussed actions to take after a breach to help you recover from any harm inflicted. The other chapters and their Tips provided you the habits to avoid common frauds from online criminals. Following the initial clean-up, there are additional steps you can take to further protect your family and yourself. When thinking through how to respond to a breach use the following mental checklist:

POST IDENTITY THEFT

When you suffer a possible or confirmed identity theft consider the following actions:

- **Prevent extended damage** by closing accounts and resetting account credentials

- **Accept any free fraud monitoring** for yourself
- **Freeze** your credit files for free at the three major credit bureaus
- **Notify your employer** / HR of the identity theft
- **Every six months** request a copy of your credit file

If you have incurred damages as a result of the breach consider the following additional actions:

- **File** a police report
- **Notify source** of breach and request remuneration
- **Hire professional** help based on severity (such as credit freezes, monitoring or full account concierge solutions)

A useful collection of online resources from a public / private partnership:

- Detailed <u>recovery steps</u> from the National Cyber Security Alliance <u>and guidance on re-establishing ownership of hacked accounts:</u>
  - » <u>https://www.staysafeonline.org</u>

It is entirely possible that someone may take over your social media account, impersonate you via your email, or worse – cost you time and money. Bad things can happen, despite your best practical applications of the tips listed in this book. Consider that even professionals who work in identity protection, computer security, and at three-letter agencies can also fall victim to these breaches.

How you respond to a breach can make a huge difference. Please seek help wherever you can from the business that was the source of the breach, from professional service providers, and from local legal avenues that are available to you!

#63 Check your Credit Report
every 4 months by cycling
through the providers

By law, in the United States, each Credit Bureau must provide annually one free credit report. Therefore, if you check with one Credit Bureau every 4 months you'll be able to receive a snapshot of your credit periodically throughout the year – for free! This is a great proactive activity to help keep an eye on your personal liabilities and financial hygiene.

THE MORE THINGS CHANGE
THE MORE THEY STAY THE SAME

The question I consistently hear from clients, family, and friends is the following:

"That is great, but what about this NEW thing here?

Technology changes at an ever-increasing speed and the burden on you to keep up with these changes is heavy and continuous. The more technology, automation, and connectedness that enter your world the more you need to adapt.

What does that mean? The first step is to follow the "Principles" shared at the beginning and through Tips within this book. They transfer nicely across all new product categories, from wearable devices to Wi-Fi connected thermostats.

By adopting these behaviors and responses, you are fully prepared to enjoy the joys of technology. Since technology changes so rapidly, I have created a Facebook site and email list to share new tips, allow Q&A on these topics, and offer reminders as we need them. You can find these tips at Facebook.com/hntbh and email update subscription service at www.hntbh.com.

ONE MORE THING ...
RULES OF THUMB TO ENJOY NEW TECHNOLOGY

- If a device <u>connects</u> to the Internet (i.e., is accessible to your smartphone), then you need to :
  - » Manage the password associated with the device
  - » Be aware that your data is being shared by the device
  - » Customize the default settings and limit the sharing of your information with other services
- If the device has a camera/microphone, be aware of privacy violation risks (i.e., block it or mute it if you are concerned)

The future looks bright with this ever-changing technology at our disposal. It allows us to share ideas, create wonderful new memories, and to live more simply. The ideal approach is not only to avoid over-complicating the technology, but also to be mindful of the potential risks

Thank you for adopting these practices in order to better yourself, better our online community, and helping sustain our way of life online.

LIST OF ALL THE TIPS

CREDIT CARDS AND SENSITIVE INFO LIFE HABITS , CHAPTER 2

1. Don't ever use your debit card
2. Swipe the card yourself
3. Always use credit cards, and preferably provide as few personal details as possible
4. No electronic transfer services attached to your debit card
5. Never pay for goods with a check or bank account online
6. If you receive any message asking for account information (banking, passwords, etc...), beware

PROTECTING YOUR MONEY ONLINE, CHAPTER 4

7. Use 'two factor' authentication for every account that has MONEY in it
8. Set up 'two factor' authentication when you move money
9. Purchase as a guest if making a one-time purchase
10. When in doubt, pay using a credit card, and... in that order

USE EMAIL SAFELY, CHAPTER 5

11. Don't open attachments in email, chat, or on phone without notice
12. Don't click on ANY links you receive!
13. Never email personal details or financial information

GETTING ONLINE - USING PUBLIC WI-FI AND KIOSKS, CHAPTER 6

14. When using a public Wi-Fi connection, confirm details with the provider
15. Do not access your bank website from a public Wi-Fi
16. Do not log onto email, social, or bank accounts from shared computers
17. Kiosks are public machines, and so is the data you give it

HOW TO BROWSE THE INTERNET, CHAPTER 7

18. Do not use Internet Explorer ever again
19. Using encryption is like wearing pants in public: it is better for everyone involved
20. When using a site... and you finish - LOG OUT
21. Challenge Questions: make up awesome fictional answers!
22. Mind your geography by recognizing the most trusted regions

SOCIAL MEDIA, CHAPTER 8

23. Be wary of random "friend" & "follower" requests
24. Do not logon onto any site with your social media account
25. Add secondary verification of identity to prevent account hijacks!
26. Share your posts and photos with true friends, but not with the 'public'
27. Disable geo-tagging on photos posted to public

SHARING AND PROTECTING YOUR PASSWORDS, CHAPTER 9

28. To make a great password use a pattern!
29. How to juggle multiple passwords: use a wallet
30. Write down your passwords
31. Change passwords annually; like bathing it is necessary eventually

32. Yes, share your passwords if you must... BUT change them within 24 hours
33. Tell your family and friends your mobile phone PIN
34. If you are sharing a password, use your phone to send it in a text message!

WHILE YOU TRAVEL, CHAPTER 10

35. When leaving your laptop or tablet on your seat to 'stretch', lock it!
36. When connecting your mobile device to a foreign car or plane, Do Not Sync
37. Turn ON a security PIN for your mobile device
38. Turn off - 'auto join Wi-Fi networks'
39. Turn off Bluetooth
40. Change the background image of device to show RETURN to me info
41. Backup your device before going on trip
42. Place electronics in the trunk before arriving in a sketchy area!

HOW TO PROTECT YOUR LAPTOP AT SCHOOL AND WORK, CHAPTER 11

43. If you are in an apartment or open work space, lock it down
44. Backups are important, but physically separate the backup from the device
45. When away, lock the screen
46. Require a password for system startup
47. Disable your web browser from remembering passwords

HOW TO PARENT ONLINE, CHAPTER 12

48. Control the Friending function
49. Disable geo-tagging

50. For anyone under 16, don't reveal last names online
51. Illicit content is on all platforms; monitor and parent what is appropriate

RECOVERING FROM A HACK, CHAPTER 13

52. Call and report lost credit card immediately
53. Never submit your username or password to a website to 'check' if it was breached
54. Request a copy of your credit report from all 3 credit bureaus
55. Regular business credit report reviews to stop illegal credit lines
56. Request a lock on your personal credit file and those of your family members
57. Create a personal copy of medical facts to protect against Medical Identity Theft
58. Refresh financial accounts with new passwords and Two-Factor verification
59. Add credit monitoring & preventive services for all members in your household
60. Replace accounts that were exposed in a crime or breach
61. Refresh online & gaming accounts to prevent loss of data and 'characters'
62. Remove embarrassing digital files

HOW TO ADAPT TO THE FUTURE, CHAPTER 14

63. Check your Credit Report every 4 months by cycling through the providers

INDEX